The Fact of Blackness

Frantz Fanon and
Visual Representation

Edited by Alan Read

D1453469

Institute of Contemporary Arts
Institute of International Visual Arts
London

Bay Press
Seattle

Honey & Rue
91.5

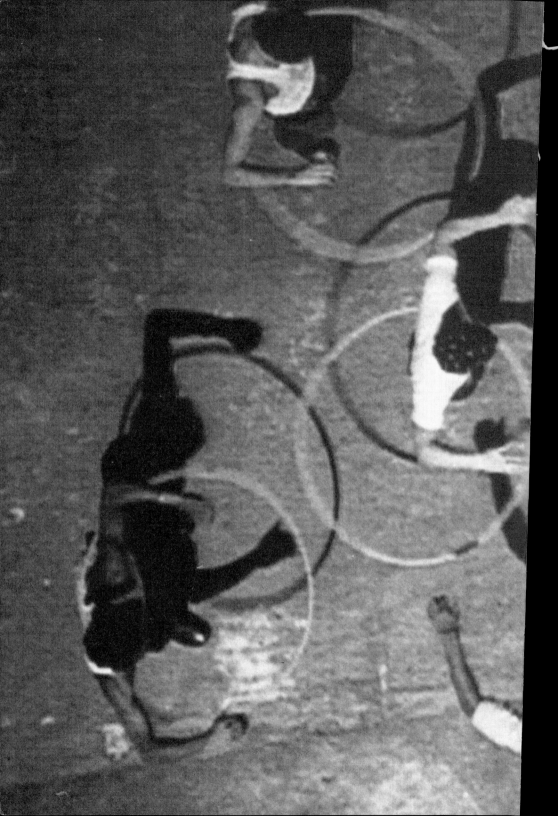

The Fact of Blackness
Frantz Fanon and Visual Representation

Institute of Contemporary Arts, London
Bay Press, Seattle

The Institute of Contemporary Arts is sponsored by
Toshiba and financially assisted by the Arts Council of
England, Westminster City Council and the British
Film Institute. Educational charity registered number
236848

ISBN Bay Press 0-941920-43-7
(USA & World rights, excluding UK & Ireland)
Bay Press
115 West Denny Way
Seattle
WA 98119-4205
USA
Tel 206 284 5913
Fax 206 284 1218

ISBN ICA 1-900300-02-8
(UK & Ireland)
ICA Publications
12 Carlton House Terrace
London SW1Y 5AH
UK
Tel 171 930 0493
Fax 171 873 0051

British Library cataloguing-in-publication data
A catalogue record for this book is available from the
British Library

Library of Congress number 96-11416

This book has been published with the financial assistance of
the Arts Council of England

and in collaboration with
the Institute of International Visual Arts

Contents

Preface

This book is intended to create a dialogue between Frantz Fanon's ideas on the significance of intellectual work, the politics of location, everyday traumas of social inequality, minorities and their experience of the contemporary metropolis, and artists and thinkers whose work has been concerned with the structures and technologies of representation, race and radicalism.

There are few figures through whom this complex of concerns could be illuminated - Frantz Fanon is one. The name of Fanon, author of seminal works such as *Black Skin, White Masks* and *The Wretched of the Earth,* is well known, yet the particular geographical and political conjuncture of his work, coupled with a radical commitment to psychiatry, remains an evocative and problematic terrain for contemporary reconsideration.

The legacy of Fanon's work provided the touchstone for *Mirage: Enigmas of Race, Difference and Desire,* an exhibition, film, live art and discussion programme which was held at the Institute of Contemporary Arts in London between May and July 1995. These events were preceded by a conference, 'Working with Fanon: Contemporary Politics and Cultural Reflection'. Artists from the building-wide project joined theorists and cultural practitioners from a diversity of disciplines to take Fanon on, to engage with each other's perspectives on his influence and to seek the resonance between their work and his work. The purpose was not to detect the effect of Fanon, but to work with Fanon in understanding how narrative, the media, image and symbol lie at the very heart of the practice of politics and social knowledge.

The Fact of Blackness is one after-effect of this work. It takes its title from a seminal chapter in *Black Skin, White Masks* which provided a provocative location for conference debate. In order to maintain the disagreements and discussions that characterised the life of the conference, dialogues have been included throughout the book which develop various aspects of the papers. The dynamic relationship between talking and doing which the *Mirage* events evoked, where the practice of artists rubbed up against the thoughts of speakers, provides another context. Yet what follows has specific additional aims: to reconsider the critical context of Fanon; to articulate the precise historical and professional milieus of his work; to discuss artists' affiliations with the nexus of race, representation and radicalism which were also Frantz Fanon's concerns; and to reiterate ways in which these concerns are already inscribed within contemporary politics.

The book moves towards looking; towards the distracted glimpse of recognition in the day-to-day encounter and the concentrated gaze of speculation in an artist's work. Looking marks the inextricable link between words, particularly those of Frantz Fanon, and the public world of sights and sounds: the common place of daily acts, which both resists and reinforces the tyrannies of injustice.

Thanks are due to the following individuals and institutions for their support of this project:

To Andrea Phillips, for working with me as editorial partner and for her dedicated management of the production of this project; to Ian Farr, co-ordinator of its production and funding; to Yumi Matote, the book's designer; to David A Bailey, without whose vision the *Mirage* season, the conference and this publication would not have taken place, and to his colleagues on the editorial advisory board, Gilane Tawadros and Catherine Ugwu; to Helena Reckitt who collaborated with me in organising the conference 'Working with Fanon'; to Homi K Bhabha who advised on the conference and chaired the proceedings; to all participants in the conference, including the audience, whose thoughts make up the heart of this book; to the Arts Council of England Visual Arts Department and Symposia Fund for funding the conference and this publication; to the Institute of International Visual Arts for collaborating with the ICA on *Mirage* and on this volume; and to the Institute of Contemporary Arts and Bay Press whose financial commitment to this book has brought it about.

We are also grateful to: Steve McQueen, Isaac Julien, Mark Nash, Martina Attille, Renée Green, Lyle Ashton Harris, Sonia Boyce, Ntozake Shange, Marc Latamie, Raoul Peck, Paul Gilroy, Thelma Golden, Sander L Gilman, Pat Hearn Gallery, Jack Tilton Gallery, the Peter Norton Family Foundation.

Alan Read
ICA Director of Talks

I

Stuart Hall

The After-life of Frantz Fanon:

Why Fanon? Why Now?
Why *Black Skin, White Masks?*

Why Fanon? Why, after so many years of relative neglect, is his name once again beginning to excite such intense intellectual debate and controversy? Why is this happening at this particular moment, at this conjuncture? And why is it around the text *Black Skin, White Masks* that the renewed 'search for Fanon' is being conducted? This essay addresses these questions as they were posed in the context of the ICA's *Mirage: Enigmas of Race, Difference and Desire*, a programme of film, installation, performance and visual art works by contemporary black artists who acknowledge some debt of influence, usually indirect, to Fanon's work. It is written in the spirit of the title of the conference which took place during the season: 'Working with Fanon'.

Why, of the many figures whose emblematic presence could have triggered off such a profusion of discursive and figural production, does the incitation turn out to be Frantz Fanon? Though at one time his name would have been widely known and recognised - usually as the signifier of a certain brand of incendiary Third World-ism - he is now virtually unknown, even amongst those young, practising, black writers and artists whose work appears, unwittingly, to betray the 'trace' of his presence. Of course, events do not obey any singular, unfolding, teleology of causality or time. But I cannot help feeling that the re-call of Fanon, now, in this moment, here, in this way, has something of the over-determined 'return of the repressed' about it - a timeliness constituted from many directions at once, as well as a certain 'un-timeliness'.

Rather than trying to recapture the 'true' Fanon, we must try to engage the after-life of Frantz Fanon - that which Jacques Derrida would call, following his recent essay on Marx, his 'spectral effect' (was *that* the *Mirage* of the title?) in ways that do not simply restore the past in a cycle of the eternal return, but which will bring the enigma of Fanon, as Benjamin said of history, flashing up before us at a moment of danger.[1] 'The colonial man who writes for his people' - that is, of course, colonial man and woman, an elision in Fanon which is as characteristic as it is un-timely - 'ought to *use* the past with the intention of opening up the future', Fanon observed; 'an invitation to an action and a basis of hope'.[2] What action, what hope is proposed to us here? And why, of all his writings, is the subject of these aspirations *Black Skin, White Masks*?

For many years it was the essay on national liberation movements in *The Wretched of the Earth*, with its invitation to the violent, self-cleansing, self-remaking anti-colonial struggle, which constituted, for many, the 'invitation to an action' - and, for others, the nightmare spectre of black barbarism stalking the streets. 'They want to take our place' is the fantasy which best seems to describe the latter response - which is how Fanon himself described the white colonial settler's 'paranoid fantasy of primordial dispossession' when confronted by the black man.[3] This contest over 'which text of Fanon's?' as a way of trying to annex his political legacy after the event is far from concluded. In his sceptical but accomplished *tour d'horizon* of recent writing on Fanon, 'Critical Fanonism', Henry Louis Gates, who is basically sympathetic to much in the post-colonial and post-structuralist enterprise, nevertheless takes some delight in exposing how varied, even internally contradictory, the recent 'readings' of Fanon as a global theorist have been.[4] On the other hand, in an essay entitled 'The Appropriation of Fanon', which savages the whole 'revisionist' expropriation of Fanon, Cedric Robinson argues that to privilege *Black Skin, White Masks* over *The Wretched of the Earth* is a motivated political strategy which, perversely, reads Fanon backwards, from his 'immersion in the revolutionary consciousness of the Algerian peasantry' to the 'petit-bourgeois stink' of the former text.[5]

It cannot be just by pure chance that it is *Black Skin, White Masks,* with its psychoanalytically-inspired exploration of the unconscious mechanisms of racism and colonialism, its attention to the role of projective fantasy, its opening up of the dislocated subjective complexity of the 'deceptively obvious "fact of blackness"' and its attention to the dialectic of identity, otherness and desire, which provides the privileged ground of Fanon's 'return' and of the contestation over him. Kobena Mercer, in his introductory essay to the *Mirage* catalogue, 'Busy in the Ruins of Wretched Phantasia', reminds us - as if we are likely to forget - that, because every reading is also a re-reading, it is bound to be political. He offers us one condition of existence for Fanon's untimely 'return': 'Whereas earlier generations privileged the Marxist themes of Fanon's later work... at the height of the optimism of the post-war social movements, the fading fortunes of the independent left during the 1980s provided the backdrop to renewed interest in *Black Skin, White Masks,* Fanon's first and most explicitly psychoanalytic text.'[6] Although there is much to this argument, it is worth recalling how, both during his lifetime and since, almost as much rhetorical energy has gone into proving how far 'Fanonism' deviated from anything like a classical Marxism. The struggle to colonise Fanon's work has been an on-going process from the moment of his death, and the identification of Fanon's writing in terms of its 'Marxist themes' in the 60s and 70s was, itself, already the product of a re-reading. As another contributory factor, Mercer cites the many-layered, discursive structure of *Black Skin, White Masks,* 'whose authorial eye constantly oscillates between multiple points of view...', and whose voice, we should add, draws on multiple registers, 'autobiographical, clinical, sociological, poetical, philosophical, political'. I will come back to the dubious proposition of some final symptomatic breaks between Fanon's early and late work, as well as to the question of how we are to re-read the multi-vocality of *Black Skin, White Masks.*

The view, boldly stated by Fanon in his introduction to *Black Skin, White Masks* - that 'only a psychoanalytic interpretation of the black problem can lay bare the anomalies of affect that are responsible for the structure of the complex' that is racism and colonialism - is what constitutes the novelty of this text.[7] But it also makes absurd the claim that 'Fanon was a political activist rather than a theorist', which those who would recuperate Fanon to some earlier, more 'revolutionary' manifestation find so seductive. Incidentally, the idea that it is only 'politics', and not also 'theory', which is at issue in these contentious readings and re-readings of Fanon is, of course, something that it suits the recuperators to have us believe, but it is not a proposition which can be seriously sustained. The problem is that Fanon's 1952 text anticipates poststructuralism in a startling way, even if the addition of the phrase: 'effective disalientation of the black man entails an immediate recognition of social and economic realities' inflects his anachronistically prescient observation in an unexpected direction. The dependency complex, he says, 'is the outcome of a double process, primarily economic... subsequently the internalization - or, better, the epidermalization - of this inferiority'.[8] A wonderful word, *epidermalization*: literally, the inscription of race on the skin. This armature of 'race' provides the black subject with that which elsewhere Fanon calls an alternative 'corporeal schema'. But, as he always insists, this schema is cultural and discursive, not genetic or physiological: 'Below the corporeal schema I had sketched a historico-racial schema... woven... out of a thousand details, anecdotes, stories'.[9]

Another deep source of the contemporary appeal of *Black Skin, White Masks* is the association it establishes between racism and what has come to be called the scopic drive - the eroticisation of the pleasure in looking and the primary place given in Fanon's text to the 'look' from the place of the 'Other'.[10] It is the exercise of power through the dialectic of the 'look' - race in the field of vision, to paraphrase

Jacqueline Rose - which *fixes* the Negro from the outside (Fanon's word, which I will use in this context) by the fantasmatic binary of absolute difference.[11] .'Sealed into that crushing objecthood...'.[12] 'Overdetermined from without...'.[13] Not only is Fanon's Negro caught, transfixed, emptied and exploded in the fetishistic and stereotypical dialectics of the 'look' from the place of the Other; but he/she *becomes* - has no other self than - this *self-as-Othered*. This is the black man *as* his [sic] alienated self-image; or as Homi Bhabha puts it, 'not Self and Other but the 'Otherness' of the Self inscribed in the perverse palimpsest of colonial identity'. It is this 'bizarre figure of desire' which, as Bhabha rightly observes, '... compels Fanon to put the psychoanalytic question to the historic condition of colonial man.'[14]

There can be little doubt that, as Gates suggested, 'Fanon's current fascination for us has something to do with the convergence of the problematic of colonialism with that of subject-formation'.[15] This bringing to bear of the post-structuralist and psychoanalytic engines of contemporary theory on the primordial - and primordially resistant - structure of racism and the historic colonial relation excites in us a disjunctive frisson of stimulation and pleasure which is only, in part, cognitive (the *jouissance* of theory having long been underestimated). Nevertheless, the familiarity of these concepts, now, may lead us to under-estimate the novelty and originality of Fanon's insights at the time of writing. The grain of his text runs incontrovertibly towards the recognition that an account of racism which has no purchase on the inner landscape and the unconscious mechanisms of its effects is, at best, only half the story. The simplistic counter-posing of *Black Skin, White Masks* to *The Wretched of the Earth*, with the implication that, in the passage from one to the other Fanon somehow 'graduated' from childish petit-bourgeois things to greater 'maturity', does not explain why *The Wretched of the Earth* ends, in the chapter on 'Colonial War and Mental Disorders', with a series of psychiatric case-studies, presented in a language which clearly echoes the paradigm first sketched in *Black Skin, White Masks*. 'Because it is a systematic negation of the other person and a furious determination to deny the other person all attributes of humanity, colonialism forces the people it dominates to ask themselves the question constantly: "In reality, who am I?" ' Fanon adds, pointedly, 'Perhaps these notes on psychiatry will be found ill-timed and singularly out of place in such a book; but we can do nothing about that'.[16] 'Nuff said.

In *Black Skin, White Masks*, this fixing of the Negro by the fantasmatic binaries of fear and desire which have governed the representation of the black figure in colonial discourse and which, Fanon argues, lie at the heart of the psychic reality of racism, is profoundly and mordantly explored. Indeed, the operation is unmasked in such a penetrating way that, in effect, we are tempted to read Fanon's text as more simple and straightforward than it is. Since the text so remorselessly returns to the binary oppositions, *black/white, coloniser/colonised*, I wonder how many of his readers unconsciously slip into reading him as if binaries are the exclusive focus of his tale? As if the real title of his book was 'Black Skin, White Skin'? Ignoring the fact that, though his subject is, of course, framed throughout by the dichotomous and manichean structure of racism as a binary system of representation and power, it is the split or divided self, the two sides within the *same* figure - the colonial Negro - which centrally preoccupies him.

The central figure of the book is the colonial Negro, especially the Antillean, who is obliged, in the scenarios of the colonial relation, to have a relationship to self, to give a performance of self, which is scripted by the coloniser, producing in him the internally divided condition of 'absolute depersonalization'.[17] The mechanisms of this substitution are very precisely described. The bodily or corporeal schema, which Fanon says is 'a definitive structuring of self and the world', necessary to any sense of self because it 'creates a real dialectic between my body and the world', is fragmented and shattered.[18] Such a scopic *gestalt*, which Jacques Lacan, for example, suggested is of great formative importance for the constitution of the subject, cannot be formed.[19] In its place, Fanon suggests, there arises the 'historico-racial schema', which *weaves him* 'out of a thousand details, anecdotes, stories' - 'battered down by tom-toms, cannibalism, intellectual deficiency, fetishism, racial defects, slave ships, and above all: "Sho' good eatin"'.[20] 'Now the fragments have been put together again by another self.'[21]

There are, Fanon insists, 'two camps: the white and the black'.[22] But, he adds, 'Overnight, the Negro has been given two frames of reference within which he has to place himself... For not only must the black man be black; he must be black in relation to the white man.'[23] The problem which preoccupies Fanon, then, is not the *existence* of the white man in colonialism, but the fact that the black man can only exist in relation to himself through the alienating presence of the white 'Other'. As Homi Bhabha correctly observes, this is 'not a neat division' but 'a doubling, dissembling image of being in at least two places at once.'[24] The subject to which Fanon addresses himself is historically specific. It is not racism as a general phenomenon but racism in the colonial relation which he dissects. His task was to unpack its inner landscapes - and to consider the conditions for the production of a new kind of subject and the decolonisation of the mind as the necessary subjective conditions for the decolonisation of the world: 'I propose nothing short of the liberation of the man of color *from himself*'.[25] It is the opening up of this radical aperture at the centre of Fanon's text which constitutes its novelty, its originality, its 'timeliness'.

Today, the question for us is how to read, how to interpret, the problem he posed, the answers which his text proposes, and the invitation to action and to hope which it prefigured?

One response has been to occupy the structure of Fanon's argument, turning the mechanisms which he identifies against themselves. This takes the question of 'the look' seriously, goes to the heart of the representational process itself, which Fanon - against the objectivist grain of the history of the analysis of racism - gave so central and constitutive a role. By the practices of trans-coding and re-signing, he attempted to contest, to disturb, to unsettle, and to re-inscribe the look 'other-wise'. Of course, for those who believe that history is a 'process without a subject', this attempt to constitute forms of subjectivity and representation in some different register from that of the colonial relation may appear to be of little serious consequence: mere scribbling in the margins. Perhaps the short history of post-colonial Algeria, in which that so-called objective entity, 'the Algerian peasantry', has been powerfully inscribed in several different and contradictory positions in the post-independence narratives, from 'revolutionary vanguard' to 'faithful multitude', may make them pause for thought. For those who take these questions of representation and subjectivity as *constitutive* of the politics of decolonisation, especially amongst the young cultural practitioners and visual artists of the African diaspora, Fanon's work has had an enormous, unpredicted, and unpredictable influence in recent years - evidence of which is to be seen everywhere in the work exhibited, screened and performed in *Mirage*. The principal counter-strategy here has been to bring to the surface - into representation - that which has sustained the regimes of representation unacknowledged: to subvert the structures of 'othering' in language and representation, image, sound and discourse, and thus to turn the mechanisms of fixed racial signification against themselves, in order to begin to constitute new subjectivities, new positions of enunciation and identification, without which the most 'revolutionary' moments of national liberation quickly slide into their post-colonial reverse gear (Algeria being one of the most troubling and heart-wrenching instances).

From this practice of resignification - this new politics of the black signifier - has flowed both the amazing volume, but more significantly, the astonishing formal diversity, of much recent black art work. Again and again, this practice has taken the form of working *on the black body itself*: driving the suppressed violence of racism so deep into itself that it reveals the transgressive lineage of the suppressed desire on which it feeds; putting together what we may think of as new 'corporeal schemas'; that which Fanon himself describes as having been fixed 'as a chemical solution is fixed by a dye', dismembered 'fragments... put together again by another self'.[26] Often, this process consists of the artist taking his or her own body as the 'canvas', light-sensitive 'frame' or 'screen', so that the work of translation and re-appropriation is literally a kind of 're-writing of the self on the body', a re-epidermalisation, an *auto-graphy*. Elsewhere, I have called this re-working of the abjected black body through desire the production of a new 'black narcissus'.[27]

The field of visual representation is foregrounded here because of the constitutive role of 'the look' as a site of power-knowledge, of the sexualisation of the gaze, and its fantasmatic fetishisation of the body and the skin as signifiers of racial difference. However, the body in Fanon's text is both a privileged and an ambivalent site of strategic intervention. 'O my body, make of me always a man who questions!'[28] In the 'epidermalization' of the racial look, Fanon tells us, exclusion and abjection are imprinted on the body through the functioning of these signifiers as an objective taxonomy - a 'taxidermy'- of radicalised difference; a specular matrix of intelligibility.

To that which W E B DuBois once referred in terms of 'hair, skin and bone',[29] after Fanon, we would have to add genitals.[30] We know that the fetishistic and stereotypical excess required to secure these markers of racial difference in a stable equivalence with the black body, far from being genetically secured, is a 'form of intelligibility' which racism shares with other regimes of difference and othering with which it has many features in common - especially, of course, gender and sexuality.[31] It is therefore sometimes tempting to believe that these are indeed the 'evidence' rather than the *markers* of difference. We mis-take their function as signifiers for their biological fact and thus read 'race' as the product of a genetic or biological schema rather than as a *discursive regime*.

Many visual practices influenced by poststructuralist and psychoanalytic ideas seem to have managed to evade a foundational materialism, only to allow 'the body' to make a surreptitious return as a sort of 'token' of the material, a terminal signifier, which brings the discursive slide, the infinite semiosis of meaning around 'race' to an abrupt halt. Sometimes, even in Foucault, who has taught us so much about its contingency, (and even more in the Foucauldeans), 'the body' seems to be invoked in the place where once stood those great transcendental signifiers, God, His Majesty and The Economy: becoming the last refuge, the *objet petit a*, of a misplaced materiality.

It is important that this work of returning to the enigmatic site of 'the black body' in the representation of radicalised difference, should not be mistaken for a return to a de-historicised, transcendental, biologically-fixed, essentialised conception of racial identity. The binary 'Manicheism delirium [*sic*]' of racialised discourse to which Fanon so effectively draws attention is not given by nature.[32] It involves an arbitrary discursive operation, a suturing. Arbitrary, because 'race' is a sliding signifier with equivalencies outside discourse that cannot be fixed. 'Racism's very rigidity... is the clue to its complexity. Its capacity to punctuate the universe into two great opposite masks... the complexes of feelings and attitudes... that are always refusing to be so neatly stabilised and fixed... All that symbolic and narrative energy... is directed to securing us "over here" and them "over there", to fix each in its appointed species place.'[33] 'Race' is not a genetic but a social category. Racism is not a biological but a discursive regime. The so-called bodily insignia - black skin, thick lips, curly hair, penises 'as big as cathedrals' and the rest - which appear to function as foundational, are not only constituted through and through in fantasy, but are really signifying elements in the discourse of racism. Even in racist discourses, where the evidence of racial difference appears to be figured so *obviously* on the surface of the body, so plain for all to see (' "Look! A Negro!" ... "Mama, see a Negro! I'm frightened!" '[34]), they are capable of carrying their negative connotations *only* because they function, in fact, as the signifiers of a deeper code - the genetic - *which cannot be seen* but which, it is believed, has the power of a science to fix and stabilise racial difference. It is not the status of racist discourse as 'scientific' but the fact that its elements function *discursively* which enables it to have 'real effects'. They can only carry meaning because they signify, through a process of displacement, further along the chain of equivalencies - *metonymically* (black skin - big penis - small brain -

Lyle Ashton Harris in
collaboration with Ike Ude
Sisterhood (1994)
unique polaroid 24 x 20",
editions 20 x 16", 60 x 48"
Lyle Ashton Harris / Jack
Tilton Gallery, New York

poor and backward - it's all in the genes - end the poverty programme - send them home!). That is, because their arrangement within a discursive chain enables physiological signs to function as signifiers, to stand for and be 'read' further up the chain; socially, psychically, cognitively, politically, culturally, civilisationally...[35]

Fanon certainly knew that, in the system of radicalised exclusion and abjection sustained by the look from the place of the Other, the bodily schema is constituted, not given, and culturally and historically shaped ('Below... I had sketched a historico-racial schema...'[36]). Thus, any notion that the return to the site of the body represents a recovery of some essential ground or foundation that will restore the essential black subject is not only mistaken but has taken a message from Fanon's work which he explicitly precludes. These are indeed, to paraphrase Judith Butler, 'bodies that matter': they count, not because they can produce the truth, but because they signify within what Judith Butler in another context calls the regulatory norm; the regulative 'ideal' of the racial matrix. How could the black body function foundationally when, as Fanon shows, it is so manifestly constructed in narrative ('there were legends, stories, history, and above all, historicity'), through desire, in fantasy, through the exorbitant play of 'lack' and 'excess'? This is surely the lesson we should take from Fanon's long and uneasy dialogue with the Negritude movement.

This body of visual work, then, assumes that 'the look' can be subverted, displaced, resisted. But can it be refused, destroyed, abandoned? Can the split - black skin/white masks - which threatens to destroy the black subject from within, be healed? Is the subject not *inevitably* a site of splitting? And if so, what then is the status of the 'universal, unified subject', beyond Negritude, towards which Fanon is gesturing in that highly resonant but ambiguous formulation at the close of his text; 'The Negro is not. Any more than the white man.'?[37]

Homi K Bhabha's foreword to the 1986 edition of *Black Skin, White Masks* has become the *locus classicus* of many aspects of this debate, reminding us that 'Remembering Fanon', as his text is called, remains a difficult and inevitably contested practice. In 'Critical Fanonism', Henry Louis Gates, borrowing a phrase from Benita Parry, critiques Bhabha's reading for its 'premature post-structuralism'.[38] Both writers mean his attempt to produce Fanon as a sort of Lacanian *avant la lettre*, as if Fanon would have taken Lacan's position on the split in the subject, and treated 'the Other' as the necessary source of division which arises in all so-called unified identities, and not 'as a fixed phenomenological point opposed to the self'.[39] Has Bhabha, then, been fishing around in that black box - Fanon's text - for all the world like a magician or a conjurer, drawing forth at the appropriate moment, to everyone's astonishment, the figure of the proverbial Lacanian rabbit?

In fact his critics, in their haste, do not always acknowledge how clearly Bhabha marks out the points in his text at which his interpretation departs from and goes beyond his Fanonian brief: 'In his more analytic mode Fanon can impede the exploration of these ambivalent, uncertain questions of colonial desire... At times Fanon attempts too close a correspondence between the *mise-en-scène* of unconscious fantasy and the phantoms of racist fear and hate that stalk the colonial scene...'[40]; 'Fanon's sociodiagnostic psychiatry tends to explain away the ambivalent turns and returns of the subject of colonial desire...'[41]; 'Fanon must sometimes be reminded that the disavowal of the Other always exacerbates the 'edge' of identification, reveals that dangerous place where identity and agressivity are twinned...'[42]. Bhabha acknowledges that, again and again, Fanon falls back too hastily onto Sartrean and Hegelian ground, is too driven by the demand for 'more insurgent answers, more immediate identifications', too hungry for an 'existential humanism'. Bhabha's real argument is, I believe, more complex. It is that Fanon constantly and implicitly poses issues and raises questions in ways which cannot be adequately addressed within the conceptual framework into which he seeks often to resolve them; and that a more satisfactory and complex 'logic' is often implicitly threaded through the interstices of his text, which he does not always follow through but which we can discover by reading him 'against the grain'. In short, Bhabha produces a *symptomatic reading* of Fanon's text. The question for us, then, is whether we should limit such a 'symptomatic reading'? With what authority, but more significantly, with what effects, do we actively appropriate Fanon's work against the textual grain?

We should be clear that what is entailed here is not a matter of restoring the 'true meaning' of the text or of fixing it once and for all in that fantasmagorical territory known as 'what Fanon really meant'. But it may be also important, in an archaeological or genealogical sense, to retrace the turns he actually took, to grasp the matrix of intelligibility within which he came to say what he did (and not say what he was unable to) and to confront its implications. For these conceptual moves and shifts had, for him then and for us now, real political consequences.

Let us put it simplistically. I think it is impossible to read *Black Skin, White Masks* without acknowledging that it is also - and not just by chance - the product of at least three inter-related but unfinished dialogues, to which Fanon kept returning throughout his life and work. First, there is Fanon's dialogue with traditional French colonial psychiatry (a much more elaborated formation than anything comparable in British colonialism, about which Françoise Vergès writes elsewhere in this volume with great insight) and within that, with psychoanalysis, Freud and the French Freudians. For, if this text is 'where Lacan makes his interruption into colonial discourse theory', as Gates asserts, it is also where Fanon 'reads' Lacan in the light of his own preoccupations. In the long footnote on the 'mirror phase', it is Fanon's *appropriation* of Lacan which strikes us most vividly.[43] First, the 'Other' in this transaction is *raced*: ('...the real Other for the white man is and will continue to be the black man. And conversely'). It is difficult not to agree that he writes here as if 'the real Other' is indeed 'a fixed phenomenological point'. Secondly, the split in the subject which the 'mirror phase' engenders, and which, for Lacan, is a *general* mechanism of misrecognition which provides the conditions of existence of all identification, is relocated by Fanon *in the specificities of the colonial relation*: 'In the Antilles, perception always occurs at the level of the imaginary... for the Antillean the mirror hallucination is always neutral [i.e. colourless]'.

This divergence is critical. On the one hand, it reminds us, as a startling discovery, how racially neutral, how strikingly *un-raced*, Lacan's discourse is, and how rarely this unmarked whiteness of his language has received comment. On the other hand, it clearly marks Fanon's distance from the logic of Lacan's position. For Lacan, as Bhabha remarks, 'identity is never an *a priori* nor a finished product; it is only ever the problematic process of access to an image of totality.'[44] To this we might necessarily add that, for Lacan, identity also operates 'at the level of the imaginary'. Fanon follows Lacan in substituting the psychoanalytic concept of 'identification' for the Hegelian concept of 'recognition'. This is a procedure which marks their common lineage in the French reception of Hegel, via the highly influential post-Heideggerean reading of *The Phenomenology* provided by Kojeve.[45] But, for Fanon, the blockage which detotalises the Hegelian 'recognition' of the One by the Other in the exchange of the *racialised* look, arises from the historically specific, specular structure of racism, not from the general mechanism of self-identification. The political implications of this deviation are highly significant. For the whole thrust of Bhabha's text - accepting a politics of subversion which lives with ambivalence, without trying to transcend or sublate it (*aufhebung*) - is the *political* consequence of a Lacanian theoretical position, where ambivalence is a necessary part of the script. Whereas Fanon's theoretical position - that this radicalisation of the 'mirror stage' is a 'pathological' condition, forced on the black subject by colonialism - has the political question of *how to end this alienation* inscribed in it. Fanon cannot, politically, 'live with this ambivalence', since it is the ambivalence that is killing him!

So, is the mechanism of misrecognition which, according to Lacan, is the condition for the formation of subjectivity in the dialectics of desire 'from the place of the Other' (implying a permanent 'lack' of fullness for the self) part of a *general ontology*, or is it historically specific to the colonial relation? Fanon's answer, at least, seems clear. 'There is of course the moment of "being for others" of which Hegel speaks, but every ontology is made unattainable in a colonized and civilized society... Ontology... does not permit us to understand the being of the black man. For not only must the black man be black; he must be black in relation to the white man. Some critics will... remind us that this proposition has a converse. I say this is false.'[46]

In fact, the strategy of Fanon's text is to engage with certain positions which have been advanced as part of a general ontology, and then to show how this fails to operate or to explain the specific predicament of the black colonial subject. What we have to confront, then, is not some mere textual or theoretical squabble between the different ways in which the Lacanian 'look from the place of the Other' is inscribed in Fanon's text and Bhabha's re-reading of it, which we can resolve by some brutal and arbitrary act of political judgement. It is a much deeper, more serious, more politically and theoretically resonant problem than that. It points to the as-yet deeply unresolved question in so-called 'post-colonial studies' as to how to reconcile - or at least hold in a proper balance - in its paradigm of explanation and reading, *both* Fanon's spectacular demonstration of the power of the racial binary to *fix*, and Bhabha's equally important and theoretically productive argument that all binary systems of power are nevertheless, *at the same time*, often if not always, troubled and subverted by ambivalence and disavowal. Our dilemma is how to *think together* the overwhelming power of the binary, which persists despite everything in all racially inflected systems of power and representation (and certainly survives their endless theoretical deconstruction); *and simultaneously* the ambivalences, the openings, the slippages which the suturing of racial discourse can never totally close up. In my view, this is inadequately resolved by subscribing to *either* position on its own. We remain between 'Bhabha's moment of discursive ambivalence and Fanon's moment of fixity'.[47]

Where did Fanon get this version of the dialectic of desire and recognition which, in a sense, he grafts on to Lacan? How did he get so deep into the Lacanian 'look', and yet so profoundly misconstrue it? These are important questions, not least because it is precisely their double register - the absence of a final resolution between them - which constitutes the excitement of Fanon's work for so many contemporary black visual artists. This question brings us to the second overlapping but unconcluded dialogue, which Homi Bhabha's account tends to underplay for obvious reasons: the dialogue of Fanon with Sartre, or more accurately, through Sartre to the ghost of Hegel, especially the master/slave dialectic outlined in *The Phenomenology*. The master/slave trope governs a great deal of Fanon's thinking in *Black Skin, White Masks,* as it did much of French intellectual thought at this time. It was in reference to the master/slave trope that Lacan said 'at every turn, I take my bearings' and it is this metaphor which opens the dialogue of otherness and desire in Fanon's text: man can be for himself only when he is a 'being-for-the-Other'.[48] It speaks especially to Fanon's concerns, not only because of its historical relevance in the master/slave form (elsewhere, it had been translated as bondsman/serf), but also because of the centrality which Hegel's account gives to the 'life-and-death-struggle' which is the final phase of the slave's struggle for recognition. For Fanon, it is the fundamental inequality, the lack of all reciprocity inscribed in the positions of master and slave, when read in the colonial relation, which opens the necessity for the slave's struggle to the death - a theme which comes to dominate Fanon's later work.

However, here again, Fanon explicitly marks his difference from a general Hegelian ontology.[49] At the foundation of the Hegelian dialectic, he argues, 'Man is human only to the extent to which he tries to impose his existence on another man in order to be recognized by him.'[50] There must be 'an absolute reciprocity... *"they recognize themselves as mutually recognizing each other"*'.[51] When this is resisted, it awakens the 'desire for recognition' and it is this which makes the slave willing to undertake a savage struggle, even to the death, since it is ' "solely by risking life that freedom is obtained" '.[52] However, for Fanon, the Negro 'slave' has never struggled to the death with the master, or staked his life. He has been *given* freedom, which is, in reality, nothing but the freedom to 'assume the attitude of the master', to eat at his table. 'Let's be nice to niggers'.[53] Once again, then, the colonial relation has interposed a specificity which *deflects* the Hegelian master/slave dialectic (just as, earlier, it inflected the Lacanian 'mirror phase') in a new direction.

In Hegel, Fanon argues, the master imposes a 'slavish work' on the slave. But in turning from the master towards work, the slave 'raises himself above his own given nature', creating himself objectively - 'voluntarily and consciously, or, better, actively or freely'.[54] However, Fanon says, in the colonial relation, the master does *not* want recognition, only work. And the slave does not abandon the master, but turns *to* him, abandoning the object. The Negro is therefore less independent in the struggle for recognition than the Hegelian slave, because he 'wants to be like the Master'. He is denied recognition, *and constructs his own being-for-himself through that denial.*

There is, however, another twist. The description of the look in the chapter on 'The Fact of Blackness' not only appropriates the Hegelian trope for Fanon's own purpose. It has also been further refracted through the existential universe of Sartre's re-reading of Hegel in *Being and Nothingness*. In Sartre, the 'look from the place of the Other' is more appropriative and possessive than the narcissistic form it assumes in Lacan. It steals the self from its in-itself. It empties the subject, a metaphor which seems only a whisper away from Lacan's 'lack' but is in fact light years away, lodged as it is in a Sartrean universe of existential scarcity. As Sartre wrote in *Being and Nothingness,* 'If we start with the first revelation of the Other as a look, we must recognise that we experience our inapprehensible being-for-others in the form of a possession. I am possessed by the Other. The Other's look fashions my body in its nakedness... By virtue of consciousness the Other is for me simultaneously the one who has stolen my body from me and the one who causes there to be a being which is my being.'[55]

I believe we can see the complex 'trace' of the master/slave trope in a number of other unexpected places in Fanon's text. I have noted the pervasive masculinist focus of *Black Skin, White Masks*. It is the question of the black *man's* desire - 'What does the black man want?' - which, as Kobena Mercer points out, triggers the text. The chapters 'The Woman of Color and the White Man' and 'The Man of Color and the White Woman' which deal with the white woman's so-called pathological desire to sleep with black men, and with the neurotic meaning, as Fanon interprets it, of the black man's desire for white women, though containing some important insights into the way projective sexual fantasies become racialised as they become gendered and racialised fantasies become 'genitalised' (rather than simply 'sexualised'), are nevertheless extremely problematic. The absence of any proper discussion of how the general dialectics of the racialised look applies, and how it may be differentiated between black men and women, is even more troubling. The way Fanon deals with the black woman when she unexpectedly surfaces in his text registers as shocking, but not unsurprising: 'Those who grant our conclusions on the psychosexuality of the white woman may ask what we have to say about the woman of colour. I know nothing about her'.[56]

Equally troubling are the passages on homosexuality (dissected at length in Kobena Mercer's essay elsewhere in this collection). It is in the context of the passage in which Fanon both acknowledges and disavows that there is any homosexuality in Martinique that he makes the astonishing remark about the 'absence of the Oedipus complex in the Antilles'.[57] The debate as to whether the Oedipus complex is culturally relative is a long-running saga. There may well be cultures where it can be shown to take another form or even not exist at all (although, far from freeing us from some Eurocentric tyranny, this usually throws us back to an essentialist biological notion of how sexual difference is constituted). But I am afraid the Caribbean is the *least* promising scenario in which to try to prove the absence of the Oedipal drama. With its son-fixated mothers and mother-fixated sons, its complex paternities common to all slave societies of 'real' black fathers and 'symbolic' white ones, along with its deeply troubled, assertively heterosexual and often homophobic black masculinities, the Caribbean 'lives out' the loss of social power by substituting an aggressively phallo-centred 'black manhood'. The absence of women and the mother in Fanon's text leads one to wonder whether, figuratively, he didn't *replace* the triadic structure of the Oedipal scenario with the binary coupling of the master/slave trope. This ambiguous 'primal scene' was beautifully transposed during *Mirage* into a different, more complex and less homophobic register in *Bear*, Steve McQueen's 1993 film of two black men locked in a playful wrestle.

Do all these Hegelian and Sartrean convolutions, matter? There are some critics who believe that the status of Fanon as a black hero and icon is damaged even by the suggestion that he might have learned anything or - worse - actually been in dialogue with the themes of European philosophy. This kind of essentialism is worse than useless if we are to think seriously about Fanon. It reveals how little such critics understand Fanon's deep implication in French culture and philosophy as a result of his French colonial upbringing, formation and education in Martinique: how much of the tortured thinking-through of the complicities of the colonial relation which was part of the impulse behind *Black Skin, White Masks* was autobiographical in inspiration. These critics forget that Fanon, like many other bright young colonial intellectuals, went to study in France; became locked in a deep internal argument with the various currents of thought which he found there; and went to North Africa as a salaried member of the French colonial psychiatric service.[58] They do not understand that, in Martinique, for many intellectuals, to be anti-colonial and opposed to the old white indigenous plantocracy was to be *for* French Republican ideology, with its rallying cry of liberty, equality and fraternity. Fanon may have travelled far from all that, but it is not clear that he ever left it all behind. The career of someone like his compatriot Aimé Césaire is incomprehensible without understanding the complexity of the relations which constituted French colonialism for black intellectuals in the Antilles.

The Hegelian-Sartrean convolutions matter in another respect. It is only in the light of Hegel's 'life-and-death-struggle' that we can understand the shadow of death which lengthens over Fanon's later work: that which he called 'the savage struggle' and 'the convolutions of death' is that which opens up the 'possibility of the impossibility'. It is death, Hegel's 'absolute lord', that makes possible the restoration of the black man's self-constituting activity, 'in-itself-for-itself'.[59] This can be seen in Fanon's commitment-to-the-death to the Algerian struggle as well as *The Wretched of the Earth*, with its in-the-shadow-of-death urgency (it was written when Fanon already knew he was dying of leukaemia) and its invocation of the necessity of violence in the revolutionary struggle for freedom.

This brings us to the third dialogue, which is Fanon's debate with Negritude, or the idea of black culture as a positive source of identification, and the question of cultural nationalism and race as an autonomous force. Fanon returns to this subject matter in *Black Skin, White Masks* in relation to Césaire, but more significantly in relation to Sartre's famous 'Black Orpheus' preface to Senghor's *Presence Africaine* anthology of African writing. The underlying issue had to do with Fanon's complex relation, on the one hand, to Sartre's 'humanist

Steve McQueen
From **Bear** (1993)
16mm b/w film
transferred onto video
Steve McQueen

universalism', which saw Negritude as a necessary transitional stage of consciousness, and on the other hand Fanon's unresolved oscillations in relation to nationalism. He was critical of nationalism as the privileged form of Third World struggle; yet he was a passionate supporter of the national cultural movement in the wider revolutionary struggle in Africa. This made Fanon, in Neil Lazarus' terms, not a 'nationalist' but a *nationalitarian*.[60] The question touches an issue of continuing controversy in post-colonial Africa and elsewhere which is probably more significant now in the wake of the crisis of the post-independence state than it was for Fanon at the time of writing; an issue whose surface was barely scratched by the ICA conference's focus on *Black Skin, White Masks*.

It was in relation to the Negritude question (which is far too convoluted to attempt to disentangle here) that Fanon wrote some of his most vitriolic phrases on the 'illusion of black culture' - and where, incidentally, one can find one of his most ambiguous and startling uses of the word 'mirage' which was the title of the ICA's project: 'with his eyes on Africa, the West Indian... discovered himself to be a transplanted son of slaves; he felt the vibration of Africa in the depth of his body and aspired only to one thing: to plunge into the great "black hole". It thus seems that the West Indian, after the great white error, is now living in the great black mirage'.[61] This was by no means his last or most definitive comment on the issue, but it is a pretty decisive one - and deeply paradoxical, as is so much of Fanon in relation to any simple cultural-nationalist appropriation of his legacy. The passages of severe criticism levelled at Césaire and Negritude in *Black Skin, White Masks* are countered elsewhere by a more sympathetic treatment. The supreme confidence with which Sartre 'placed' Senghor's collection as 'transitional' in relation to a universal humanism did not rest easily in Fanon's mind. He never resolved the tensions between these two claims.

I find myself in agreement, on this point at least, with Benita Parry's recent insistence on Fanon's 'persistent instabilities', on the unresolved arguments and the incomplete oscillations which make *Black Skin, White Masks* fundamentally an *open text*, and hence a text we are obliged to go on working *on*, working *with*. In particular, I am pulled back to Fanon's many voices as the sign of the multivocality of the dialogue going on in his head, which came to no settled conclusions. Parry proposes that *Black Skin, White Masks* is Fanon's 'learning process', a kind of journey of self-education and self-transformation without the solace of an arrival.[62]

I agree, then, with the reasons which Homi K Bhabha advances for the importance of *Black Skin, White Masks* at this conjuncture. He characterises Fanon's text as a 'jagged testimony of colonial dislocations' which in the end 'refuses the ambition of any total theory of colonial oppression'. In my reading of the text, Fanon *is* more consistently drawn to 'the question of political oppression' in a specifically colonial historical context as 'the violation of a human "essence"' than Bhabha suggests. This refrain is textually insistent, central to his evolving political vision, less a 'lapse into... a lament in his more existential moment' than Bhabha allows. But I also agree with Bhabha about Fanon's insistence on exploring the question 'What does the black man want?' to its depths. This question, as enigmatic and unconsciously charged as Freud's 'What does woman want?', nevertheless pushes us to that dangerous point, beyond the limit, where 'cultural alienation bears down on the ambivalence of psychic identification'.[63] This is a place many 'right-on' critics are determined to avoid. Fanon's insistence on thinking this dangerous moment in terms of fantasy and the desire-for-the-Other transforms our notion of politics and of political demands. The question is, what are we to do with the 'uncertain dark' which Bhabha suggests is always the accompaniment to the emergence of truly radical thought?

Does 'working with Fanon' require that we undertake a symptomatic re-reading of *Black Skin, White Masks*, re-sighting through the aporias in his text a conceptual scheme which is somehow struggling towards enunciation; a 'going beyond' of the text to that absent-presence which it implicates but cannot name? Or should we acknowledge that he did not name it because, though uncannily closer to it in more ways than many of his followers and subsequent critics have understood, he is also more distant. Racism is never, for Fanon, simply something which the Other does to Us. His thinking about it, though finally unresolved, is shaped by an appropriation of some ideas that significantly depart from and in some respects explicitly contradict the place from which we tend to 'read him' today. This requires us to live with a much more radically incomplete Fanon; a Fanon who is somehow more 'Other' to us than we would like, who is bound to unsettle us from whichever direction we read him. This also requires us to engage with the uncomfortable truth that just as 'truly radical thought never dawns without casting an uncertain dark', so there is no 'life' without its after-life.

1   See Walter Benjamin, 'Thesis on the Philosophy of History' in *Illuminations* trs. Hannah Arendt (Fontana, London 1973) p 247.

2   Frantz Fanon, *The Wretched of the Earth* (Grove Press, New York 1966) p 69.

3   Homi K Bhabha, 'Remembering Fanon', foreword to Frantz Fanon, *Black Skin, White Masks* (Pluto Press, London 1986) p. xv.

4   Henry Louis Gates, 'Critical Fanonism' in *Critical Inquiry* vol 17 no 3 Spring 1991.

5   Cedric Robinson, 'The Appropriation of Frantz Fanon' in *Race and Class* vol 35 no 1 July/September 1993.

6   Kobena Mercer, 'Busy in the Ruins of Wretched Phantasia' in *Mirage: Enigmas of Race, Difference and Desire* (ICA/inIVA, London 1994).

7   Frantz Fanon, *Black Skin, White Masks* op cit p 12.

8   Frantz Fanon, *Black Skin, White Masks* ibid p 13.

9   Frantz Fanon, *Black Skin, White Masks* ibid p 111.

10 See Sigmund Freud, *On Sexuality*, Pelican Freud Library vol 7 (Penguin, Harmondsworth 1977).

11 See Jacqueline Rose, *Sexuality in the Field of Vision* (Verso, London 1986).

12 Frantz Fanon, *Black Skin, White Masks* op cit p 109.

13 Frantz Fanon, *Black Skin, White Masks* ibid p 116.

14 Homi K Bhabha, 'Remembering Fanon' op cit p xiv.

15 Henry Louis Gates, 'Critical Fanonism' op cit p 458.

16 Frantz Fanon, *The Wretched of the Earth* (Grove Press, New York 1966) p 203.

17 Frantz Fanon, *Toward The African Revolution* (Penguin, Harmondsworth 1970) p 63.

18 Frantz Fanon, *Black Skin, White Masks* op cit p 111.

19 See Jacques Lacan, *Four Fundamental Concepts of Psychoanalysis* (Hogarth Press, London 1977).

20 Frantz Fanon, *Black Skin, White Masks* op cit p 112.

21 Frantz Fanon, *Black Skin, White Masks* ibid p 109.

22 Frantz Fanon, *Black Skin, White Masks* ibid p 10.

23 Frantz Fanon, *Black Skin, White Masks* ibid p 110.

24 Homi K Bhabha, 'Remembering Fanon' op cit p xvi.

25 Frantz Fanon, *Black Skin, White Masks* op cit p 10. Emphasis added.

26 Frantz Fanon, *Black Skin, White Masks* ibid p 109.

27 Stuart Hall, '"Race" - The Sliding Signifier' in *Race, Ethnicity and Diaspora* (Harvard University Press, forthcoming).

28 Frantz Fanon, *Black Skin, White Masks* op cit p 232.

29 W E B Dubois, 'The Conservation of Races' in ed. Howard Brotz, *Negro Social and Political Thought* (Basic Books, New York 1966).

30 Fanon quotes Michael Cournot as saying that 'Four Negroes with their penises exposed would fill a cathedral'. See *Black Skin, White Masks* op cit p 169.

31 Judith Butler, *Bodies That Matter: On the Discursive Limits of Sex* (Routledge, London 1993).

32 Frantz Fanon, *Black Skin, White Masks* op cit p183.

33 Stuart Hall, 'Race, Culture and Communication' in *Rethinking Marxism* vol 5 no 1 Spring 1992.

34 Frantz Fanon, *Black Skin, White Masks* op cit p 112.

35 For an elaboration of the discursive character of racism, see Stuart Hall, '"Race" - The Sliding Signifier' op cit.

36 Frantz Fanon, *Black Skin, White Masks* op cit p 111.

37 Frantz Fanon, *Black Skin, White Masks* op cit p 231.

38 See Benita Parry, 'Problems in Current Theories of Colonial Discourse' in *Literary Review* no 6 Winter 1987 and Henry Louis Gates, 'Critical Fanonism' op cit.

39 This is rather in the way that Althusser and Balibar in *Reading Capital* used structural concepts to 're-read' Marx in his partially theorised state, to produce - hey, presto! - the fully structuralist Marx.

40 Homi K Bhabha, 'Remembering Fanon' op cit p xix.

41 Homi K Bhabha, 'Remembering Fanon' op cit p xx.

42 Homi K Bhabha, 'Remembering Fanon' op cit p xxii.

43 Frantz Fanon, *Black Skin, White Masks* op cit p 161.

44 Homi K Bhabha, 'Remembering Fanon' op cit p xviii.

45 See A Kojeve, *Introduction to the Reading of Hegel* (Basic Books, New York 1969).

46 Frantz Fanon, *Black Skin, White Masks* op cit p 109-110.

47 B Hall, *Reading the Mulatta*, unpublished thesis, University of York (1995).

48 See ed. J Forrester, *The Seminars of Jacques Lacan, 1* (Cambridge University Press, Cambridge 1988) p 222.

49 Frantz Fanon, *Black Skin, White Masks* op cit p 220 footnote 8.

50 Frantz Fanon, *Black Skin, White Masks* ibid p 216.

51 Frantz Fanon, *Black Skin, White Masks* ibid p 217.

52 Frantz Fanon, *Black Skin, White Masks* ibid p 218.

53 Frantz Fanon, *Black Skin, White Masks* ibid p 220.

54 A Kojeve, *Introduction to the Reading of Hegel* op cit p 229.

55 Jean-Paul Sartre, *Being and Nothingness* (Citadel Press, New York 1969).

56 Frantz Fanon, *Black Skin, White Masks* op cit p 179-80.

57 Frantz Fanon, *Black Skin White Masks*, ibid p 180 footnote 44

58 See Françoise Vergès, 'Chains of Madness, Chains of Colonialism: Fanon and Freedom' in this collection.

59 Frantz Fanon, *Black Skin, White Masks* op cit p 218.

60 See Neil Lazurus, 'Disavowing Decolonisation' in *Research In African Literatures* vol 24 no 4 Winter 1987.

61 Frantz Fanon, 'West Indians and Africans' in *Towards the African Revolution* (Penguin, Harmondsworth 1970) p 37.

62 See Benita Parry, 'Signs of the Times' in *Third Text* no. 28/29, Autumn/Winter 1994.

63 Homi K Bhabha, 'Remembering Fanon' op cit p xi.

Dialogue

Homi K Bhabha
Stuart Hall
bell hooks
Gilane Tawadros
Members of the audience

Bhabha   Do you think that the question of the new humanism has a particular relevance for us now in thinking about what people refer to as the 'transnational'?

Hall   I do think that in the transnational, globalised context in which these ideas have now to be thought that the question of humanism comes back in a different place. When one refers to humanism in the context of Fanon's own moment, one reads it as if it means something rather different. It emerges in the complex and unresolved thinking about nation. He would not let go of the idea of nation, and gave his life to a struggle which defined itself as a national liberation struggle. He was deeply critical of those aspects of the nation that were simply a celebration and recuperation of the past, nonetheless he insisted on the moment of the particular, the moment of the national, as the necessary condition for something wider - something international. This is a very complex rethinking of the relationship between the national and the international that I don't think has been picked up anywhere before. There is now coming into existence an easy postnationalism - 'the nation is always a structure of power, a structure of exclusion' etcetera. We forget how central it was, in Fanon's moment, precisely as an emancipatory project.

hooks   Stuart, I am interested in whether you would add a dialogue about gender to the three dialogues you have initially proposed, because it seems to me that Fanon is writing gender through race in some ways.

Hall   I deliberately did not include gender because it is dealt with at length in Kobena Mercer's essay with which I substantially agree. I do say some things about gender and sexuality, which are problematic in Fanon, but I'm not sure I'd call it a 'dialogue' which Fanon takes on. I think it is one of the dialogues that Fanon does not take on in the same way in *Black Skin, White Masks*. Of course, it is there, but it does not seem to me to be one of the things with which he is consciously wrestling. The other dialogues are ones he knows he's wrestling with: he's using their language, trying to squeeze them to mean something else. I think the passages on homosexuality and the passages on relations between men and women are a blind spot.

hooks   I don't see them as a blind spot, I see them as a calculated refusal. That's why I see it as a certain kind of dialogue. I am trying to disrupt this sense that we should refuse to place gender in any moment.

Audience   Homi Bhabha, at the beginning of this conference you said that the event was not going to be a ceremonial or memorial for Fanon. I think it has become both those. You have managed to move Fanon from politically committed to some sort of trendy postmodern bullshitter. That's because you are assuming a type of discontinuity between Fanon of the 50s and 60s, between the man who wrote *Black Skin, White Masks* and the man who wrote *The Wretched of the Earth*. The continuity in his discourse however shows itself more than once. His political relation to the Third World is still alive. It is wrong to assume a different Fanon.

Bhabha   I situated my introduction within *The Wretched of the Earth*. I sought to take specific passages, all of which came from moments when Fanon was talking about the history of the Algerian struggle, and to relate them to what is obvious to us here as another political agenda, one that is not the same as that. I think there is another location of those texts in a very different context. I don't think that by focusing on *Black Skin, White Masks*, Stuart Hall in any way gave a postmodern soufflé of the subject - where the lightness of its being becomes the criteria of its success. Stuart Hall engaged with the theories of Hegel, Sartre, Lacan and Freud precisely to re-politicise the contemporary moment. We may have very different readings of what the political imperative is in the contemporary moment.

Audience   Homi Bhabha, can you relate the concept of transnational humanism to your use of Levinas and ethics in philosophy? Is there a link in the way that you are using them?

Bhabha   I think so. I am currently working on what I call 'unsatisfied universals'. I'll put it briefly: there is one way of thinking about the universal in philosophy which talks about the universal and its failure. Out of that emerges a set of ethical theories. I am interested in the moment when you have to posit a universal in an unsatisfied condition, and the unexpected transformations that emerge as a result of this. To give an example, Fanon says that there is a continual need to talk about the totality of the event. But in the middle of talking about the totality of the event he always talks about those other moments: he says 'how do I totalise the event if I try and think about bringing a past tradition - a past insurgent tradition - into the cultural war, when I know that the tradition has completely changed'. It is this contingent transformative moment in a citation of the universal which sets up a site which neither is nor is not universal, but which is a partial identification.

Tawadros   I want to come back to the idea of national consciousness which is not nationalism, as a bridge to the international or transnational. This comes out of a specific historical moment of colonial struggle. Is it possible to have a national consciousness now which is not about nationalism without that specificity of the colonial struggle?

Hall   I don't have an answer to that. The reason is because we are in the middle of what Homi Bhabha would call 'transience' in relation to questions of the nation. That is, an attempt to dismantle a structure we think we know, whose negative features we will become aware of in time. I was referring earlier to the inevitably two-sided ambivalence of the structure we call a nation, and the complicated relationship between things that are national and nationalism. There is a need to break down some of these equivalencies. There has been a failure of certain hopes in Third World struggles. Today we have to think that moment outside of, and against the frame of, a constituted nation which has been precisely the form of the deformation of that open objective. It is perfectly clear why it is that we now bring to bear, collect and mobilise very negative feelings about it. One has the feeling that this cannot possibly exhaust the variety of identifications and discourses which are required to operate in the complexity of the present conjuncture. After all, we know that the transnational and the global themselves are layered in a complex way, and we know that they do not consist of any simple transnational, overriding, subsuming, hegemonising and homogenising of difference, but precisely the proliferation of difference. It is the re-articulation of global and local which is going on, not the obliteration of the local by the global. If you think about it in those terms, wish as you may, some of the things that reside institutionally and ethically at the level of the nation will not simply be wiped away because we have become disillusioned with it as a political form. The nation is still a palpable, complex and contradictory reality. We can't think about the present conjuncture without thinking a bit more than we have about the question of what constitutes the national in relation to the international. Why is it that Fanon could not let go, subscribe to or celebrate this question unequivocally? What is he arguing with in his passages on Negritude? He's arguing with Sartre about whether that notion of an empty international humanism is viable any longer when forms of political struggle consistently take the national form. He can't get past that fact and keeps changing his mind about it. That's what takes us back to this question of the nature of the so-called transnational in an era when nations still persist, which seems to have slipped so easily from a negative to a positive register while passing through exactly the ambivalent middle point with which it really engages.

Bhabha The national boundary has become re-cathartic, and every claim to transnationality is some negotiation with an international territory which produces unexpected transformations. The use of new technology, for instance, or the use of certain camera angles which produce new epic texts. There is one particular kind of moment that is very important: the national in the Fanonian 'good' sense can be found in those kinds of minority fronts, which are articulating a transnational connection, outside of the usual currency of national discourse. For instance, an issue around AIDS or certain ecological movements gets transnationalised in a way that is not to forget the national boundary but to question how to negotiate it: a national group against the patriotism of its own nation territory which wants to make a link with other issue-based minorities who are equally ambivalently placed with their national spaces. It is that minority as the agency of transnationality which I think is very important.

Hall It should not be forgotten that in the tumultuous period after decolonisation in the 50s and 60s, which was punctuated time and time again by the action of national liberation movements, the Algerian war has a very special and distinctive place. It was the decolonising war in which torture of the civilian population was practised as it had never been practised before. The colonial wars which followed, which made use of torture by the military forces, learned from the experiences of the French army in Algeria. It is not possible to understand the reverberations of the question of violence in Fanon's work, particularly in *The Wretched of the Earth*, without understanding this. Also, the French army was a conscript army, unlike, for example, the professional French army that was used in the Indo-Chinese war. In Algeria, those conscripts were being educated in the practices of systematic violence on men and women of the liberation struggle.

All of the wars in the decolonising period had profound reverberations in the colonial metropolis. The moment that the French army was defeated, or faced defeat in Algeria, brought the war 'home'. Was this the coup - the take-over - by the defeated troops of France itself? Algeria was very close - 'just across there', 'just the other side of the Mediterranean'. This mythic closeness gives North Africa in general, and Algeria especially, a particular place in the French imaginary. The

Le Pen movement in France today can be seen as part of a long revenge for the decolonisation of French North Africa. The idea that this decolonisation process has no contemporary resonance is simply not the case. It is absolutely present in new forms in the current history of Europe.

Colin Salmon as Frantz Fanon
Production still from **Frantz Fanon:
Black Skin White Mask** (1995)
Dir. Isaac Julien
Prod. Mark Nash
Normal Films
Photography by Elspeth Collier

Françoise Vergès

Chains of Madness, Chains of Colonialism:

Fanon and Freedom

Fanon and Freedom

> Within one week after his appearance Fanon was carrying out
> what are still regarded as feats. He had interviewed as many
> doctors and nurses as he could when he first arrived. He asked
> them what their ideas of mental illness were, and he made it
> clear that unlike his predecessors he did not regard his role as a
> passive one. He meant to be a working doctor and teacher, for
> Blida was not only a hospital but a teaching institution. As in
> other hospitals of the day, at Blida patients considered seriously
> ill or dangerous were confined to their beds by being tied to the
> springs. When Fanon saw this he wasted little time in changing
> the situation. He walked through the hospital wards unchaining
> men and women, informing them that hence-forward they
> would be free to walk and talk, to consult with him and with
> other doctors and nurses. The effect was electric. Those who
> were witnesses to the event recall it as a historic day for Blida.[1]

This story, told by Irene Gendzier in her biography of Frantz Fanon,
constructs the mythic figure of a liberator. The image of Fanon
walking through the wards, 'unchaining men and women', is
powerfully evocative. As readers, we become the spectators and
witnesses of a scene set in a French colonial mental hospital, in which
the hero is a black man who does not hesitate to overturn the colonial
medical and social order. We imagine Fanon, dressed in his white coat,
walking with the authority and legitimacy of a psychiatrist, a *Chef de
Service*, entering these wards in which the wretched are chained. This
symbolic gesture of removing chains takes on an even greater meaning
when one thinks that these chains evoke the chains of slavery which
had been forced upon Fanon's ancestors by French men. Now, this
descendant of slaves is shown liberating men and women from their
chains in land in northern Africa colonised by French men.

It does not matter whether this story is true or not. Narratives which
reconstruct the birth of a new era tend to tell a story in which, in a
corrupted or degraded situation, a man emerges and with the power
of his will and his humanistic concern, radically transforms the
situation. This transformation is inaugurated by a gesture, a
declaration, an unexpected act, which ruptures the past and impresses
upon its witnesses the thought of a new beginning. The narrative
about Fanon removing chains contains, in its projective
representation, decolonisation, emancipation, freedom from the chains
of madness and freedom from the chains of colonisation, all
powerfully linked together.

According to psychiatric interns who worked with Fanon at Blida-Joinville, patients were not tied or chained.[2] They were, as in any other Western or colonial mental hospital of the day, locked in cells and abandoned to their own devices. If patients became too excited, straitjackets were used to impede their movements.[3] The 'psychoactive revolution' had not yet occurred, and the range of available drugs was narrow.[4] Fanon, an advocate of institutional therapy, certainly opposed violent methods. Nevertheless, he was a psychiatrist of his time, who used chemical psychiatry, electro-shock therapy, or straitjackets when other means of restraint had failed or when he felt that the condition of the patient required it.[5] Testimonies have confirmed, however, that he transformed his ward at Blida.

I am not interested in a quarrel about the veracity of this scene. What I want to explore is its symbolic representation, and with it, Fanon's own conception of madness and freedom. To Fanon, man constructs his own history, free from the chains of both alienation and desire. Man must seize his freedom and be free to act, to choose. This freedom demands mastering one's life, one's desire, one's position in society. Madness is one of the obstacles to freedom; a *temporary* loss of consciousness which is not fatal. 'Fanon wanted freedom, total freedom, to free man from his chains, all his chains', a friend has said.[6] To Fanon, there is a continuity between individual and political freedom and freedom from all that hinders full and free consciousness. Individual alienation and political alienation are related; both are the product of social, political, and cultural conditions that must be transformed. His conception of madness owes both to his philosophical views and to the radical reassessment of psychiatry after World War II: his practice harks back to Etienne Esquirol's conception of the asylum as a therapeutic tool.[7]

The narrative of Fanon unchaining the patients evokes the gesture of Philippe Pinel, the French doctor and founder of modern psychiatry, who liberated the insane of the hospital of Bicêtre from their chains during the French Revolution. As with Pinel, the narrative is there to illustrate a rupture between two epochs. Pinel broke with the classical notion of madness, transforming the mad into the sick;[8] Fanon broke with the colonial-racial notion of madness. Contradicting the idea that men were imprisoned in their madness, outside human communication, Pinel affirmed that the insane still had the capacity to reason and that the therapist had to appeal to the intellectual faculties, the feelings and *passions* of the insane. With him, the 'idea of an alienated individual whose presence of mind and reflection are purely and simply abolished was rejected'.[9] Pinel developed a new conception of madness, 'inseparable from a general idea of man, and especially from man's conscious power of choosing'.[10] The legend of Pinel liberating the patients from their chains - for it was a legend - has obscured his theory which inaugurated modern psychiatry.[11] The myth has operated as a screen.

How could we not make a parallel between Pinel and Fanon? Pinel worked at the time of the French revolution and its promise of liberty and equality; Fanon worked at the time of a particular struggle for national liberation and its promise of liberty and dignity. In both events, the dream had liberty as an imperative, linked to ideals of a 'new man' and a 'new society', along with the desire to build a present upon the erasure of the past. Fanon as the committed political activist, risking his life in the struggle for national liberation, has influenced the representation of Fanon as a man, a French Martinican and a psychiatrist who broke with all the premises of psychiatry. In our post-antipsychiatry and post-Foucault moment, psychiatry has acquired a bad reputation for disciplining and punishing; as a scene of racism and indifference to sexual and cultural differences, especially in the colony. But Fanon took the role of psychiatrist seriously and tried to apply its most recent discoveries and techniques in the post-colony. It is important to situate Fanon's practice within psychiatry, to show that his approach belonged to a reformist psychiatric movement, which postulated the full humanity of mental patients. To examine his work as a psychiatrist is to acknowledge his affiliation with a psychiatry which assigned to the asylum the function of 're-socialisation' (mental alienation being a 'de-socialisation').

Concerning the 'logic of madness', Fanon hesitated between optimist and activist psychiatry founded on a *médecine de la personne* [medicine of the subject], and oriented himself toward relieving suffering and reintroducing man to his freedom. He had much sympathy for Lacan's thesis that 'madness, far from being an "insult" to freedom, is his most faithful companion, following him like its shadow'.[12] In his thesis, in a discussion about the respective theories of Henry Ey and Jacques Lacan on madness, Fanon concluded that the *social aspect of human reality* remained to him essential.[13] Psycho-somatic medicine attracted him, and he remarked: 'Psychoanalysis has a pessimistic view of man. The care of the person must be thought as a deliberately optimistic choice against human reality'.[14]

Fanon's psychiatric practice at the hospital of Pontorson, Normandy (September 21 to November 22 1953), at the hospital of Blida-

Joinville in Algeria (1953 to 1956), at the hospital Charles Nicolle in Tunisia (1957 to 1959), and in the military camps of the ALN on the Algerian-Tunisian border, has to be examined in its historical and theoretical context.[15] Fanon brought to the colony the practice of the most progressive school of French psychiatry - the school of institutional therapy - and added to its insights his understanding of the psychological consequences of racism and colonial domination. One could see a parallel between the historical context of Pinel's innovation, revolutionary France, the abolition of the monarchy, the creation of a republic in which men, even the insane, are all born equal, and, two centuries later in the colony, the historical context of Fanon's innovation, the project of abolishing feudal colonialism and founding a republic in which men, even the insane, will all be born equal. At the hospital of Blida, the pride of the mental health colonial system in Algeria, he opposed the colonial discourse on 'Muslim pathology' and affirmed that Muslim men were human beings who deserved to be taken seriously and respected. Thus Fanon ruptured the colonial psychiatric practices that had dominated the discipline since around 1910. He claimed that, if the psychiatrist ignored certain social and cultural realities when treating mental patients, he would find himself in an impossible situation. Indeed, if the goal of psychiatry was to 'enable man no longer to be a stranger to his environment',[16] if the work of the psychiatrist was to reconcile the sick man with his social environment, then how could a psychiatrist do his work when the environment rejected the very social and cultural values of the individual? To send Muslim patients back to a world which denied their symbolic order in a process of dehumanisation would constitute a negation of Fanon's conception of his role as a psychiatrist.[17] Fanon would liberate the insane as he would liberate the wretched of the earth.

In France, reformist psychiatrists fought against the regression of the conditions of living and care in the asylum. In the colony, this regression had been compounded by racism and ignorance of the native culture. Two revolutionary gestures were thus necessary: a Pinelian gesture which would restore the patients to their full humanity and a political gesture that would strike down a feudal colonial system. Both gestures were needed in order to achieve a revolutionary situation. But the revolution inaugurated by Fanon maintained madness within psychiatry. To him, madness was the 'other' of consciousness and his role was to restore the patient to his consciousness. Madness was worked out through the logic of reason.

'Reason must be opposed to the de-reason of the patient. One cannot be sick with a healthy brain, with neat neurone connections; thanks to these connections, a way is opened *through which the doctor must enter with new principles*' Fanon said in 1959 at the University of Tunis.[18] His psychology was a sociology of mental disorders. Yet, this approach did not justify serving society if this society was oppressive. Fanon denounced the psychiatrists who, during the war, collaborated with the French police and army. He criticised notions of 'native psychology' and 'basic personality'.[19] But again, his discourse about madness remained contained within a social and political perspective. To Fanon, crimes, mental disorders and melancholia among Algerians were the *direct* product of the colonial situation. The novels and poetry produced by Algerians at the same time revealed a more complex approach to the violence of the encounter between a colonial Christian society and a Muslim and pagan world, as well as a more complex approach to Algerian society and its own violence. On one hand, it is because these approaches existed that we can today reassess Fanon's perspective without seeing it as anachronistic. On the other hand, it would be too easy to charge Fanon with a lack of awareness of the diversity and complexity of Algerian society when anthropological or sociological research was still dominated by the colonial school. Fanon, his friends have said, exhibited a great curiosity for the Algerian culture and customs. He went to Kabylie to observe the local healing practices and the rituals against 'possession' and always advocated a humanistic psychiatry.[20] He thought that the Pinelian psychiatric revolution which had occurred in Europe could be applied to the non-European world, where the enemy was not classically defined madness but its colonial version. Colonial psychiatry had said that madness was *a fact of nature* in the Muslim population. Islam had made the Algerians 'idiotic'. Fanon's daring gesture was to oppose this conception, replacing nature with society. Colonialism had made the Algerians 'mad', he said. The cure was political emancipation. To the conception of madness as temporary chains upon one's consciousness, Fanon added his political anti-colonialism (- armed struggle will break the chains of colonialism) and his philosophical view (- man must be free of the chains imposed by culture and society).

Madness and culture

When Fanon arrived at Blida-Joinville, a year before the beginning of the war for national liberation, the majority of colonial society still divided the world between 'civilised Selves' and 'un-civilised Them'. Fossilised in their views, colonial social scientists ignored the transformations experienced by the social sciences in France and Europe after World War II. Psychiatry continued to speak with the vocabulary of colonial psychiatry.

Colonial psychiatry was heir to both the school of degeneration, which in the West had influenced all the psychiatric discourses from the middle of the nineteenth century to the beginning of the twentieth century, and social Darwinism. Benedict Augustin Morel claimed in his influential work *Traité des dégénérescences physiques, intellectuelles et morales de l'espèce humaine* (1857), that he would describe the 'mode of production of degenerated beings, their classification, hygiene and treatment'. The laws of heredity became of central concern to the adherents of degeneration. Theories which had emerged about the potential madness of the 'dangerous classes' - the anarchist, the communard and the vagabond - were extended to the colonised. Gustave Le Bon, in *Les lois psychologiques de l'évolution des peuples* (1894),[21] proposed the notion of 'psychological race', which was in direct lineage with Gobineau's racist theory and influenced a generation of psychologists. Le Bon, who was an advocate of polygenesis, made a connection between gender and race, arguing that 'proof of female inferiority, and of similarities between women and Negroes, was provided by craniology'.[22] To him, 'each people possesses a mental constitution which is as fixed as its anatomical characters', and 'each individual is not only the product of his parents, but also, and in fact above all, of his race, or, in other words, of his ancestors'.[23] Race was imprinted on memory. Léopold de Saussure pursued Le Bon's approach in his *La psychologie de la colonisation française dans ses rapports avec les sociétés indigènes* (1899). De Saussure, who was against the 'moral ideals of assimilation' because they did not 'take into account racial heredity',[24] wrote that:

> The acquisition of shared mental characteristics creates veritable 'psychological races'. The psychological characteristics are as stable as the anatomic characteristics, upon which a classification of the species was made. Psychological characteristics are reproduced, with regularity and constancy, like anatomic ones, through heredity.[25]

Algeria quickly attracted the interest of the medical gaze. In 1907 Boigey, a physician of the French army, complained about the indifference to cultural and religious aspects of the Muslim patients and pleaded for a hospital with a mosque in which trained native doctors and nurses would work.[26] The same Boigey however developed a thesis about 'Muslim pathology' a year later in which he argued that Islam was both a cause of madness and a prevention against madness.[27] But it was Antoine Porot who organised the service of psychiatric assistance in Algeria.

Porot, who had opened the first modern psychiatric ward in Tunisia in 1912 (where, 40 years later, Fanon would open the first day-care psychiatric hospital), was nominated *Médecin Chef* of Algiers in 1916.[28] The psychiatric hospital of Blida-Joinville, where Fanon would be a *Chef de Service*, was built under his direction.[29] Porot was the founder of the *Ecole d'Alger*, whose main thesis was that the non-European brain had a pathological constitution. In a 1918 article, Porot argued that the Muslim showed no emotion, was credulous and stubborn, superstitious and stuck in childhood, passive and exhibited an indifference to the future, and had no ability for moral thinking.[30] He asserted that, 'The native Muslim shows a remarkable propension for passivity; static personality, as we have said, hinders in him the dynamic personality'.[31] Porot insisted on the importance of mimicry among the Muslim population but warned that the effects of such 'discordance' should be seen as 'troubles caused by mimicry', rather than 'psychotic symptoms'.[32] The Muslim population has remained in infancy, he wrote, and yet its puerile thinking was not similar to that of European children, because Muslims lacked their sense of curiosity and comparison. The Muslim was devoid of any of the characteristics that defined the European (who was an entrepreneur with a scientific curiosity; a sceptic and secular individualist). The Islamic religion was accused of maintaining Algerians in a state of credulity and superstition, of being a factor of illiteracy, ignorance and xenophobia.[33] Yet, alongside their exhibition of arrogant superiority, these colonial writings contained some observations about Algerian society which have proved durable: for instance, the importance of the group in the individual's life, the importance of religion and the place of the father or male ancestor in the social organisation. Porot's approach showed a concern shared by ethnologists and historians: what was the place of culture and the past in the making of psychological traits? As Jean-Michel Bégué has argued, Porot, his predecessors and his disciples raised questions which have remained central to ethno-psychiatry or trans-cultural psychiatry. Their theses were an attempt to establish, against scholars in the metropolis, an 'indigenous' school which would found its authority and legitimacy upon their knowledge *in situ*. They had the right to speak because they 'knew' the natives, 'understood' their customs, religion, traditions:

they wanted the 'natives' well-being', but their knowledge came to better use in the colonising project. They were the products of the French Republic, persuaded that serving the republican ideal was serving the whole humanity. Colonial civil servants, whether coming from France or the Old Colonies,[34] often exhibited the greatest devotion to the secular ideal in which progress and science constituted the pillars of civilisation. The main thesis of the *Ecole d'Alger* - the natural inferiority of the Muslim population - had a lasting influence upon psychiatry in Algeria. New schools of anthropology and the psychoanalytical revolution had no impact upon colonial social sciences. The latter certainly felt threatened by the universalism of these discourses since their thesis rested on an insistence upon difference. Raymond Berthelier, in his study of the history of psychiatry in Algeria and Philippe Lucas and Jean-Claude Vatin, in their study of colonial anthropology, have noted how the colonial social sciences shut themselves away from changes in the metropolis.[35] Yet, to Berthelier, Porot was not an exceptional man but a 'man of his time', who shared the 'civilising ideal' which dominated French politics and culture, promoting an 'ideology of difference' which justified a politics of colonial domination. The entire population of Algeria and its culture became pathologised; the objects of the European psychiatric gaze. Colonial psychiatry with its sociocentric and ethnocentric vision was a political project rather than a way of apprehending madness.

Colonialism and madness

The revolution introduced at the hospital of Blida-Joinville by Fanon and his interns Jacques Azoulay, Alice Cherki, Charles Geronimi and François Sanchez, aimed to deconstruct the representation of the North African subject developed by Porot and his school. They tried to apply two principles: the hospital as a site of conviviality and social interaction rather than a site of exclusion, and institutional therapy. The first principle had been developed by Esquirol, the successor of Pinel, who said that an asylum was an agent of recovery, and that in the hands of a clever doctor, it could be the most powerful therapeutic agent against mental disorders.[36] This conception of the asylum emerged after the French Revolution and was contemporary to the theory of 'moral treatment', which recognised the existence of subjectivity and reason in the mental patient. The project was to reconstruct in the asylum a social environment in which the values of discipline, work and self-restraint would be taught to the patients through pedagogical methods. Though this utopian project ran quickly into financial, theoretical and practical difficulties, and patients were often punished, locked in their cells, and abandoned, its ideal remained alive. Criticisms against the degradation of the asylums, renamed psychiatric hospitals in 1923, cleared the way after World War II for a radical reassessment of this 'therapeutic tool'. In this reformist movement, the school of 'institutional therapy' was influential.

'Institutional therapy' designated both a new relation between the therapist and his patients and a transformation of the hospital into a convivial place. A group of therapists launched the first experience of institutional therapy at the psychiatric hospital of Saint-Alban, which came to embody the theory and practice of this school.[37] Fanon, who became a training intern at Saint-Alban in 1952, fully embraced this approach and greatly admired one of its theorists, François Tosquelles, who became his mentor and his friend.[38] Tosquelles was a Catalan who, during the Spanish Civil War, reorganised the psychiatric service of the republican army.[39] A refugee in France in 1939, he opened a psychiatric service in the concentration camp of Septfonds, before being offered work at the hospital of Saint-Alban in January 1940.[40] Tosquelles transformed Saint-Alban, which was directed by Paul Balvet, into an experimental site for his theory.[41] The goal of institutional therapy, Tosquelles said, was 'essentially to structure and transform the psychiatric hospitals so that a real psychotherapy would be possible'.[42] The practice of group therapy was central because this form 'suited best the fact that patients lived together, worked and had a good time together'. Since life in the hospital encouraged group behaviour, this social form was integrated into the therapeutic project. Influenced by the techniques of psychodrama and group therapy developed in the United States, the psychiatrists of the school of institutional therapy talked of the hospital as a *clinique d'activités*. They insisted on the necessity of working with the nurses and with the patients in non-hierarchical groups. The role of the psychiatrist was carefully delimited as that of helping the group without imposing interpretations. The space had to be organised around the social reality of the patients. Workshops and group activities would happen in the living rooms, so that 'even the idle patient would be induced to participate in the common activities'.[43] The patients would be paid for their work according to their 'normative cultural model and to respond to a concrete social need', and they would be entrusted with organising a theatre and writing and producing a newspaper. In summary, institutional therapy wanted to 'humanise the psychiatric asylum'.[44]

The school of institutional therapy considered that psychoanalysis could not respond entirely to the needs of mental patients. The 'group' constituted by the psychiatric doctor, the nurse, and the patients was the primary unit. Collective interpretations were preferred. 'Everything must occur within the framework of social groups, in order to avoid any personal interpretation being given to the individual', Georges Daumezon wrote. The mental patient was, to the psychiatrists of institutional therapy, first and foremost an '*aliéné*, a man who had broken the social contract by becoming an alien to the social milieu, a man excluded from social life, a "de-socialized" man'.[45] The goal of institutional therapy was to re-integrate the patient into society.

> The obstinate and irreducible sociality of the *aliéné* is his unique anchor... It represents the therapeutic 'door' which psychiatric medicine must exploit to its greatest point. One must believe in the biological nonsense of madness to apprehend madness as an error. One must speak up for the *aliéné* against himself, speak up for his social *chance* against the appalling fatality of his destiny.[46]

Yet the return to society was not a passive return. Institutional therapy intended to act upon society and as Daumezon explained:

> The goal is to re-open the patient toward society: we have a contradiction here, because society was among the conflicting factors, its structure is itself torn. Therefore the doctor can direct the patient toward this return only by giving him the means to 'assume this split', that is to fight against it. Life in the hospital must thus lead the patient toward an acting behavior against these internal contradictions and prepare him, when he leaves, to an *existence of conscious struggle* [*une existence de lutte consciente*].[47]

Fanon fully adopted the vision of institutional therapy. His ambition was to apply its principles and to add his own observations to its theory. He always tried to duplicate the experience of Saint-Alban.

Saint-Alban represented not only a haven for the excluded - those marginalised from 'normality' - but also a haven for those who defended the marginalised and wanted to transform society; a haven for political activists. Indeed, during World War II, Saint-Alban served as a refuge for wounded resistance fighters, as Blida would serve as a refuge for the wounded fighters of the Wilaya IV.[48] Fanon remained faithful to the principles of Saint-Alban. Thus in the course which he taught at the University of Tunis in 1959 - 1960, entitled 'Rencontre de la société et de la psychiatrie', he exposed his theory of madness and recovery along the lines of an activist institutional therapy. 'The insane is an "alien" to society and society decides to exclude this anarchic element'. Fanon questioned the established criteria of normality and added: 'To be socialised is to answer to the social milieu, to accept that the social milieu influences me'.[49] After considering the workplace and its production of mental disorders, Fanon indicted racism, its production of guilt and desire of whitening, of overcompensation, and self-destruction: 'Blacks often have only one resource; to kill'. This led Fanon to raise the 'problem of the encounter' in colonised society. The pathologisation of the colonised was the projection, Fanon argued, of the colonisers' own pathology. 'Is the colonial lazy?' Fanon asked, and answered: 'The laziness of the colonised is a form of protection; and foremostly a measure of self-defence on a physiological level'.[50] His conclusion was: 'The colonised person who resists is right' ('*Le colonisé qui résiste a raison.*'). The argument moved from the insane as alien, excluded from his society, to the colonised alienated, excluded from his own society. The necessity in both cases was to break the chains of alienation.

Institutional therapy and culture

Fanon applied the principles of institutional therapy in theory and in practice. In the wards under his direction at Blida-Joinville, Fanon organised group therapy, meetings with nurses and the staff, and reading groups with the interns.[51] Jacques Azoulay's thesis tells the story of this experience.[52] Following a long introduction in which institutional therapy is explained and advocated, Azoulay exposed the problems and difficulties that they confronted when trying to apply institutional therapy to Muslim men. Group therapy, occupational therapy and other activities had worked well with women, but Muslim men resisted any attempt to interest them in these activities. Nurses contradicted the doctor's orders; 'Patients remained passive and nurses interpreted these meetings as chores'. Azoulay exposed the trials and errors of Fanon and his interns and their effort to understand why and where they had failed:[53] 'How could we realise a sociotherapy inspired by Western elements in a Muslim ward? How was a structural analysis possible if we grouped together the geographical, historical, cultural, and social frameworks of a society?' Fanon and Azoulay described Muslim society as a theocratic society in spirit, with Islamic beliefs dominating the social life from civil laws to morals, science and philosophy, and family behavior; a gerontocratic society in which the father ruled with absolute authority, and an ethnically complex society, organised as well along class divisions. These remarks about the social and cultural organisation of Muslim society constituted the foundations upon which Fanon reconstructed the theory of institutional therapy for a non-European hospital. Re-opening the mosque was more important than asking the patients to participate in the theatre since they were in majority religious and men to whom theatre was a 'feminine' activity; making them cultivate a garden with jasmine and vegetables was more suited to their skills and images of themselves than asking them to weave baskets; opening a *café-maure* with Arabic music, tea, and games of dominoes had more effect than asking illiterate men to become interested in a newspaper; respecting Muslim holidays and inviting an imam responded better to their needs than inviting them to celebrate Christmas; bringing in a storyteller brought together men who had repelled group therapy. Fanon went against a tradition among the psychiatrists of the *Cadre Français* which displayed a passivity towards the organisation of living conditions at the hospital and an indifference towards local conditions.[54] He showed that Muslim patients were not condemned to unresponsiveness and convinced nurses and interns of the necessity of transforming the hospital into a 'machine to cure the patients'.[55]

The assumption in institutional therapy that the group was *naturally* therapeutic, that individuals *naturally* rediscovered among others their sociality and their desire to live again among others testified to an optimism which did not take into account the difficulties of social life. Colonialism and its violence, its disruption of traditional life, of family life and of economic organisation, was responsible, Fanon said, for the majority of mental troubles. But if colonialism acted as a manichean device, it also acted as a 'screen' obscuring the complexity of social organisation. In other words, the world which appeared to Fanon as the 'Muslim world' was itself a construction. Since the experience was essentially aimed at transforming the hospital and adapting the principles of institutional therapy to a non-European society, there were few observations about the multiple sources of mental troubles. Rather, *one* source was blamed: colonialism.

Though the experience at Blida was revolutionary, it did not offer a study of the causes which had led each individual to this place. The male patients were in majority poor *fellahs*, agricultural or unskilled workers. What had led them to the psychiatric hospital was, Fanon and Azoulay explained, the impossibility of finding a place in a society disrupted by colonisation. As farmers, as peasants, as unskilled workers, they had no place in an economy based on capitalist efficiency and in which large mechanised farms had replaced small family farms. Yet, was this phenomenon peculiar to Algeria or akin to that which had occurred in the metropolis, where rural men had suffered in a similar way from economic modernisation? Did proletarianisation cause mental disorders? Were the patients sick because unemployed and poor, or because they were colonised, or both? Did the patients experience mental troubles because of family problems or sexual problems? Women had answered well to institutional therapy but why were they in hospital? Why were the two main groups in the psychiatric wards European women and Muslim men?[56]

Peasants, poor, dispossessed men appeared victims of a world in which 'the abstract violence of money exercised its power. The peasant and the native were now defined as the opposite of the ruler. Only the latter was "*notable*", that is, could be located in a scale of values established by himself, which was said to be the scale of *humanity*.'[57] Outside the scale of this so-called 'humanity', the poor peasants, the natives, the women, became 'mad', or killed 'to make themselves heard'.[58] The men, who constituted the majority of the patients at the asylum both in the metropolis and in the colony, were those rejected by the modernisation of the economy and agriculture: illiterate men, bearers of an oral culture in a world in which the written word, the word of the law, and of administration, were the words of French men. However, in the colony, this modernisation of masculinity was accompanied by ethnocentric thinking. Muslim men were 'backward' not only because they were illiterate peasants but also because their civilisation, culture, and religion was backward-looking.[59] Colonial psychiatry had maintained that colonised men were prone to hysteria; that they suffered from a disease that was marked with its relation to femininity. They killed for no reason. The colonisers contrasted a reliable, modern, responsible and protective construct of masculinity to this 'colonised masculinity' that was unreliable, violent and immature. Fanon answered this dichotomy by arguing that there was a relation between colonialism and masculinity (in its psychological sense) which entailed a profound destabilisation of the colonised. He remarked that masculinity was a fragile construction (he had explored the fragility of this construction among Antillean men in *Black Skin, White Masks*), that colonialism had configured colonised masculinity as feminised and emasculated, and concluded that men in the colony had to reconstruct their manhood and their freedom through a rejection of colonial images. If colonised men killed, their crimes were the expression of passive resistance against an order that had crushed them. In his denunciation of the colonial psychiatric diagnosis of the criminality of the North African - 'a reaction written into the nature of things, of *the thing* which is biologically organized'[60] - Fanon situated the sources of alienation in the *social organisation* of colonialism. His insistence on the necessity for cultural relativism in the psychiatric diagnosis and treatment of non-European peoples confirmed the concerns of ethnopsychiatry. His solution was to offer a tyrannical ideal for colonial men, tyrannical because it established a superego that demanded the avoidance of ambivalence, weakness and ambiguity. He saw decolonised masculinity as emulating virile, militarised qualities. Colonialism prevented colonised masculinity from becoming modern by branding it with the mark of the pre-modern. Decolonised masculinity would be modern and heroic. Fanon countered the taxonomy of colonialism with new categories. He contested a narrative that mocked masculinity through dehumanisation. The solution, he insisted, was the construction of a 'new man'. The images of the native soldier holding up against the colonial soldier, of the native leader defeating the colonial governor were powerful ones. Yet, phallic masculinity, as it was deployed through war or moments of intense political mobilisation, sustained the construction of a fearless, courageous masculinity but undermined the foundations of a new, decolonised masculinity. The images and stories linked to heroic masculinity tended to hide the more complex ways through which colonised men answered to the colonial hegemonic discourse. The heroic soldier and the fearless leader were tropes that set up as their opposite the unheroic, weak man, who implicitly belonged to the colonial past. Fanon's binarism - hero or passive accomplice - foreclosed on masculinity and imprisoned its expressions within virilism.[61] The male colonised Muslim provided Fanon with the heroic masculine figure, but the great absent figure was the enslaved African man, the ancestor of Martinicans, defeated and deprived of his name, his paternal function.

History, memory and freedom

Fanon wrote, 'The body of history does not determine a single one of my actions. *I am my own foundation.*'[62] In his clinical observations he had noticed the effect of history, but its chains were in contradiction with his conception of freedom. His psychiatric practice was always oriented toward a recovery of 'freedom'. In his final experience, at the opening of the first day-care hospital in Tunisia in 1959, Fanon further developed his conception of the hospital as a fundamental therapeutic tool.[63] Though institutional therapy was still attractive, Fanon thought that it did not fully offer 'freedom', this essential component of life. The danger was to recreate a micro-society in the hospital and thus, finally, reinforce the institution of the hospital rather than destroy it.[64] The solution was a day-care hospital, so that the patient's life would remain integrated in its family and social environment. 'The supreme characteristic of a day-care hospital is the complete freedom it provides the patient, breaking completely with the relative, and sometimes absolute, coercion which being locked up constitutes' Fanon wrote.[65] Mental pathology constituted, he said, a 'veritable pathology of freedom'.

To Fanon, psychiatry was auxiliary to the political struggle for freedom. Psychiatry had a political goal. The past acted as an obstacle to freedom. Fanon thought that decolonisation had to be the *tabula rasa* of a world cut in two; that it was 'quite simply the replacing of a certain "species" of men by another "species" of men', an 'absolute substitution'.[66] 'There is no real creativity' under colonial domination, Fanon argued at the Second Congress of Black Writers and Artists in 1959. Hybridity and syncretism were impossible intellectual positions: 'The intellectual who is Arab and French, or Nigerian and English, when he comes up against the need to take on two nationalities, chooses, if he wants to remain true to himself, the negation of one of these determinations.'[67] The 'disappearance of colonialism was also the disappearance of the colonised', and only the creation of the nation would 'give life, in the biological sense of the term, to national culture'. Any analysis that would read colonial history as a discontinuous chain of ambivalent and subversive moments, rather than as a series of decisive moments of rupture, would mask the reality that the colonial world is the 'murderous and decisive struggle between two protagonists.'[68]

The rejection of imperialism's signifying system, proposed by Fanon, supposes that the possibility exists of creating an entirely new one. Such a project begs questions of this new signifying system's conditions of formation. Fanonian theory depends on a system which organises history as a progressive development. It implies that women and men have the power to reinvent their symbolic and material world; to shed memories. Fanonian theory construes memory as a series of lifeless monuments, a morbid legacy, a melancholic nostalgia for a past long gone. There is no place for dreams, for inventing a future. Memories are shackles to progress and movement. There is in this approach a fantasy of self-engendering, of refusing an affiliation in which it is impossible to receive and to transform.

Fanon wanted revolution to be a creation, unfettered by the spirits of the past that burden the living with past losses and defeats. Revolution would be a means to negate these defeats. Yet he did not discuss what was the *foundation* of his society, the Creole society of Martinique, and the *defeat* that slavery had been. A past of slavery, Toni Morrison has said, 'until you confront it, until you live through it, keeps coming back in other forms. The shapes redesign themselves in other constellations, until you get a chance to play it over again'.[69] This moment - this 'loss' - was constitutive of the present. The recognition of this loss was part of the process of becoming other, an 'other' whose subjectivity was not contained in colonial representation, but transformed by its experience of colonialism. In other words, rejecting the self of colonisation, when one was subjected to the humiliations of colonialism, rejecting the shame produced by that moment, might be constructing a fantasmatic original innocence, spoiled by colonialism.

Nicolas Abraham and Maria Torok have proposed a distinction between *conservative repression* and *constitutive repression* that offers a way out of the dilemma between melancholic memory and repression. *Constitutive repression* is dynamic repression, in which there exists a 'desire that seeks its way through detours and finds it in symbolic realizations'.[70] In *conservative repression* the past is buried, neither transformed into ashes nor capable of being retrieved. The past weighs on the present, solidified in denial and disavowal. It hides a secret. What is repressed? A crime. What crime? Slavery. With what words can this crime be told? Slavery was 'indigestible and unabsorbable, completely. Something that has no precedent in the history of the world, in terms of length of time and the nature and specificity of its devastation'.[71] The fear is that if the repression of this history is lifted, there is the possibility of more horror. Horror was, but no longer is, the narrative says. Why would one insist in showing the wounds, in bringing back this 'tragedy'? To awaken the nightmare? How to put this crime on trial, a crime whose *reality* weighs on the present?

Abraham and Torok have remarked that if the epistemological alternative lies between suppressing the reality of the crime and refusing the judicial system because it is arbitrary and relative, there is no way out. The participants in the crime would remain incapable of recognising their participation and accept a historical reality in its complex and multifarious expressions. The world is then like a grave, inhabited by ghosts whose presence haunts the living. Opening the grave, freeing the ghosts, mourning the dead would be a start in the processes of anamnesis.

Anamnesis, the work of thought, is a different process to *tabula rasa* or morbid melancholia. One can start from the assumption that the 'past has the value of representing what is lacking [*ce qui fait défaut*]'. A group can express what is still lacking, or still to come, only through a redistribution of its past. From the knowledge of the past, of the conditions that made it such, a group can decide what is lacking, for instance freedom or equality. History is always ambivalent, for the 'place it gives to the past is equally a means to open the way to the future'.[72] Michel de Certeau warns that, because of this ambivalence, this significance of a lack, historical analysis may vacillate between conservatism and utopia, reactionary and revolutionary politics. Yet, as he concludes, one can understand both these limits and the potential of ambivalence, a symbolisation of the limit and the possibility of going beyond this limit.[73] There is a 'form of retroaction: the past as projective', which 'is not a cyclical form of repetition that circulates around a lack'.[74] The projective past, Homi Bhabha argues, 'introduces into the narratives of identity and community a necessary split between the time of utterance and the space of memory. This "lagged" temporality is not some endless slippage; it is a mode of breaking the complicity of past and present in order to open up a space of revision and initiation'.

Revising the history of decolonisation through the Fanonian perspective opens up the questions of symbolic decolonisation, the place of psychiatry in the post-colony and of masculinity. Fanon thought that psychiatric practice could answer to the problems of mental health. The technique of the day-care hospital, though 'developed in countries with high economic development could be transplanted in a so-called under-developed country without losing any of its value'[75]. Colonised men were constructed in the legal, medical, and psychiatric colonial discourse as feminised, weak, emasculated men: decolonisation was the conquest of political and cultural freedom. That institutional psychiatry was also thought to recover masculinity was not surprising, and Fanon insisted that emancipation was also psychological. Yet that which was offered through the orthodoxy of the Algerian narrative about decolonisation - a narrative that Fanon supported and developed - was militarised virility.[76] The sons, betrayed by the fathers who had not stood up against colonialism, would incarnate a virile manhood, erase a past of humiliation and mend the wounded masculinity of the native man. But Kateb Yacine had warned that the ancestors tend to return to avenge themselves with ferocity. Fanon's messianic message, with its Christian tone and revolutionary romanticism, produced a powerful, yet ultimately flawed discourse about emancipated masculinity. Fanon proposed an autonomous self, uninhibited by the ties of desire and love, except for the abstract love of the undifferentiated oppressed. His work as a psychiatrist belongs to the history of the reformists who, confronted with the suffering of mental patients, sought to alleviate their condition and offer them solace and a place among their social fellows.

Throughout this essay, I have deliberately used the term 'man' and the pronoun 'he'.

I would like to thank the ICA, Homi K Bhabha, Catherine Hall, Stuart Hall, Alan Read, and all participants in the ICA conference Working with Fanon for their suggestions and criticisms. My collaboration with Isaac Julien and Mark Nash for the realisation and production of a documentary, *Frantz Fanon: Black Skin, White Mask* (Normal Films for BBC Television, December 1995) was also extremely fruitful.

Frantz Fanon
Archival photograph
courtesy Olivier Fanon
Film still from **Frantz Fanon:
Black Skin White Mask** (1995)
Dir. Isaac Julien
Prod. Mark Nash
Normal Films

1   Irene L Gendzier, *Frantz Fanon: A Critical Study* (Pantheon Books, New York 1973).

2   Discussion with Jacques Azoulay, Alice Cherki, and François Sanchez, July 1995.

3   In 1790, Guilleret, a tapestry-maker of the hospital of Bicêtre, invented the straitjacket. Chains were progressively abandoned following this invention. Cited by Jacques Postel, D F Allen and A Mousnier, 'Pinel à Bicêtre de 1793 à 1795', in ed. Jean Garrabé, *Philippe Pinel* (Les empêcheurs de penser en rond, Le Plessis Robinson 1994) p 43.

4   After the Second World War, therapeutic drugs used in psychiatry were the same as those used before the war. A new era for therapeutic drugs opened in 1952 with the use in psychiatry of the drug chlopromazine. In less than eight years, a whole series of new drugs were discovered, and it was around 1965-1970 that many patients were able to leave psychiatric hospitals.

5   See his argumented defense of the method of Bini (electroshock therapy) in an essay written with François Tosquelles, 'Sur quelques cas traités par la méthode de Bini', *Congrès des Psychiatres et Neurologistes de Langue Française* (LI, Pau 1953) pp 539-544.

6   Charles Géronimi, Radio show about Fanon (INA Archives, n.d.).

7   On post World War II psychiatry see: Bertrand Foutrier, *L'Identité communiste... la psychanalyse, la psychiatrie, la psychologie.* (L'Harmattan, Paris 1994); Jacques Postel, *Genèse de la psychiatrie* (Le Sycomore, Paris 1981); Jacques Postel and Claude Quetel, eds., *Nouvelle Histoire de la Psychiatrie* (Dunod, Paris 1994); Elizabeth Roudinesco, *Histoire de la Psychanalyse en France,* *Volume II* (Seuil, Paris 1986); François Tosquelles, *Éducation et psychothérapie Institutionnelle* (Hiatus Edition, Mantes laVille 1984).

8   See Michel Foucault, *Folie et Déraison. Histoire de la Folie à l'âge classique.* (Plon, Paris 1961) and *Naissance de la Clinique* (Quadrige, PUF, Paris 1963); ed. Elizabeth Roudinesco, *Penser la Folie* (Galilée, Paris 1992).

9   Gladys Swain, 'De l'idée morale de la folie au traitement moral' in *Dialogue avec l'insensé.* (Éditions Gallimard, Paris 1994) pp 85-109.

10 Ibid p 93.

11 On this legend see Gladys Swain, *Le sujet de la folie. Naissance de la psychiatrie* (Privat, Toulouse 1977).

12 'Loin qu'elle soit pour la liberté "une insulte", elle est sa plus fidèle compagne, elle suit son mouvement comme une ombre', Lacan wrote in *La causalité essentielle de la folie.* This quote was cited by Fanon in his thesis.

13 Frantz Fanon, 'Altérations mentales, modifications caractérielles, troubles psychiques et déficit intellectuel dans l'hérédo-dégénération spino-cérébelleuse', unpublished Thesis in Medicine, University of Lyon, 1951. In his thesis, Fanon showed that he was an interested reader of psychoanalytical theory.

14 Cited in *L'information psychiatrique 51* (no 10, December 1975) p 1090.

15 The Armée Nationale de Libération [National Army of Liberation] was the organized army of the Algerian nationalists.

16 Frantz Fanon, 'Letter to the Resident Minister (1956)' in *Toward the African Revolution*, trans. Haakon Chevalier (Grove Press, New York 1967) pp 52-54.

17   See Fanon's letter of resignation in which he wrote: 'What is the status of Algeria? A sytematized de-humanization... The events in Algeria are the logical consequence of an abortive attempt to decerebralize a people' ibid p 53.

18   'La raison doit être opposée à la déraison du malade. On ne peut être malade avec un cerveau sain, avec des connexions neuroniques nettes; à travers les connexions, il y a une sorte de voie ouverte à travers laquelle le médecin doit s'introduire avec des principes novateurs.' Frantz Fanon, 'Rencontre de la société et de la psychiatrie. Notes de cours, Tunis, 1959-1960'. (Université d'Oran: Études et Recherches sur la psychologie en Algérie-CRIDSSH, n.d.) p 3.

19   See Fanon's articles 'Medicine and Colonialism' in For a Dying Colonialism, trans. Haakon Chevalier (Grove Press, New York 1965) pp 121-146; 'The North African Syndrome', in Toward the African Revolution opcit pp 3-16; and 'Colonial War and Mental Disorders', in The Wretched of the Earth trans. Constance Farrington (Grove Press, New York 1966).

20   Testimony of Jacques Azoulay, July 4, 1995.

21   Gustave Le Bon, Les lois psychologiques de l'évolution des peuples (Félix Alcan, Paris 1894). Le Bon's works, written around the time of the Dreyfus Affair, were translated into some ten languages and sold hundreds of thousands of copies.

22   Cited in Tzvetan Todorov, On Human Diversity, Nationalism, Racism, and Exoticism in French Thought, trans. Catherine Porter (Harvard University Press, Cambridge MA 1993) p 114. Originally, Nous et les autres (Éditions du Seuil, Paris 1989).

23   Le Bon, Les lois psychologiques de l'évolution des peuples op cit p 6 and p 13.

24   Léopold de Saussure, La psychologie de la colonisation française dans ses rapports avec les sociétés indigènes (F. Alcan, Paris 1899) p 37.

25   Ibid p 14 and p 38.

26   Algerian patients were sent to metropolitan asylums until 1938.

27   Boigey, 'Etude psychologique sur l'Islam', Annales Médico-Psychologiques, vol 8, October 1908 pp 45-67. On the history of psychiatry in Algeria, see Jean-Marie Bégué, 'Un siècle de psychiatrie en Algérie (1830-1939)', unpublished Master in Psychiatry, University of Paris-Saint Antoine, 1989 and Robert Berthelier, L'Homme Maghrébin dans la littérature psychiatrique (L'Harmattan, Paris1994). On psychiatry in the French colonial empire, one should read the report presented in 1912 by Emmanuel Regis and Henri Reboul, 'L'assistance aux aliénés aux colonies' in Rapport au XXII Congrès des médecins aliénistes et neurologistes de langue française, Tunis, 1-7 Avril 1912 (Masson, Paris 1912). This 218 page report is remarkable for its detailed advocacy of the institutionalisation of psychiatry in the colony. It clearly exposes the project of colonial psychiatry. Regis and Reboul advocated a. the training of doctors specialized in colonial psychiatry, assisted by native doctors and nurses, b. the application in the colonies of the 1838 law, c. the creation of specialized hospitals, and d. an effort against alcoholism which plagued the colonised. Regis and Reboul went against the notion that madness did not exist among 'primitive societies' but insisted that: 'Only a doctor who knows not only Arabic but also the normative

mentality of the Arabs, their customs and mores, is really apt to understand the Arab's mental pathology and therapeutically acts upon it'. See also Henri Aubin, 'L'assistance psychiatrique indigène aux colonies', *Congrès des médecins aliénistes et neurologistes de langue française* (Alger, 1938) pp 147-162.

28 Porot would become the first professor of neuro-psychiatry at the *Faculté de Médecine* at Algiers. On Porot and the *École d'Alger*, see Sleïm Ammar, 'Antoine et Maurice Porot à Tunis', *Psychologie Médicale* (1983 15:10) pp1717-1718; Bégué, op cit; Berthelier, 1994, op cit, and 'Psychiatres et psychiatrie devant le musulman algérien', *Psychopathologie Africaine* (980 16:3) pp 343-369. See also the thesis of two students of Porot: D C Arrii, 'De l'impulsivité criminelle chez l'indigène algérien', unpublished Thesis of Medicine, University of Algiers, 1926, and Suzanne Taieb, 'Les idées d'influence dans la pathologie mentale de l'indigène nord-africain. Le rôle des supersititions', unpublished Thesis of Medicine, University of Algiers, 1939. Antoine Porot was the artisan of the construction of the psychiatric institution in Tunisia and Algeria. A doctor in the colonial army, he first observed the specific 'mental troubles' of the colonial troops that had been sent to fight for France during World War I. He left Tunisia for Algeria in 1922 with his two children, Colette and Maurice, who both would become psychiatrists. Maurice practised in Algeria at the Clinique Saint-Raphaël in the borough of El Biar at Algiers, which had been founded by his father. Maurice Porot left Algeria at the independance in 1962. During the war, he wrote articles about the psychological consequences of the Algerian war, published in the *Annales Médico-Psychologiques*, which are worth reading for the clinical cases he presents. Though Maurice Porot never gave a direct opinion about the war, his choice of words for the Algerian nationalists, 'terrorists', 'fellaghas', and his deliberate neutral scientific position could be taken as the expression of a political position.

29 In 1852, the first asylum was opened in the French colonial empire on the island of Guadeloupe, followed in 1881 by the asylum at Ile de Nou (New Caledonia), in 1885 by the asylum of Martinique and 1912 by the opening of an asylum in Madagascar and Tunisia. The architecture of the hospital of Blida-Joinville, constructed in 1916, followed the architecture of colonial hospitals elsewhere: a two-storey building with large windows, set in a park. Blida-Joinville was opened in 1938 and visited by the psychiatrists and neurologists present at the Congress of Alienists which was taking place at Algiers that same year. We must note that the construction of colonial psychiatric hospitals happened more or less at the same time as the construction of psychiatric hospitals in France (for instance, the asylum in Marseille opened in 1844).

30 Antoine Porot, 'Notes de psychiatrie musulmane', *Annales Médico-Psychologiques* (May 1918, 10: 9 pp 377-384). See also: Antoine Porot and D.C. Arrii, 'L'impulsivité criminelle chez l'indigène algérien-ses facteurs', *Annales Médico-Psychologiques* (December 1932, 14:2 pp 588-611). It was the conclusions of the 1932 article which Fanon attacked in his chapter 'Colonial War and Mental Disorders' in *The Wretched of the Earth*.

31 'L'indigène musulman a une propension remarquable à la vie passive; chez lui, comme on l'a dit, la personnalité statique étouffe la personnalité dynamique' Porot, 1918 p 380.

32 Ibid p 382. In a long footnote, Porot criticized the psychiatrists who diagnosed 'negativism', 'psychosis', in Muslim patients who, for instance, have refused to eat simply because it was Ramadan. Colonial psychiatry was not 'blind' to cultural difference, it was culturalist *and* universalist, a patronising mixture of concern and contempt.

33 Porot's writing exhibits the characteristics of a discourse that was popular in France at the time: contemptuous of religious beliefs (progress and science demand the rejection of these beliefs) and of rural traditional life (peasants are credulous, backwards), and partisan of hygiene and prevention (campaigns against alcoholism, promiscuity). We could find in metropolitan France quite similar representations of the peasants of Brittany or of the working-class population. I do not want to romanticize the life of these groups, but I want to point to the arrogance of a discourse that claimed to be truthful. Further, this form of discourse, when applied to the natives in the colony, took a tragic dimension in a situation of extremely violent military conquest, genocide, and dispossesion of land.

34 The Old Colonies were the colonial empire constituted before the French Revolution: Guyana, Guadeloupe, Martinique and Réunion Island. In these colonies, a plantation economy, slavery and métissage constituted the matrix through which the population and its culture emerged. The elite of these colonies,

white Creoles or persons of color, provided the French colonial empire of the Third Republic with a class of committed civil servants. Their children, who had access to French universities after World War II, often turned to anti-colonialist struggle. Fanon was the son of a Martinican civil servant, who was a freemason. (The role of the freemasons in the colonies would deserve a whole study. They were republicans, often opposed to the abuses of colonization, defending a 'republican colonisation' which would bring 'progress, science, and secular education' to the empire).

35 Berthelier, op cit; Philippe Lucas and Jean-Claude Vatin, *L'Algérie des Anthropologues* (François Maspéro-Fondations, Paris 1975).

36 Une maison d'aliénés est un instrument de guérison; entre les mains d'un médecin habile, c'est l'agent thérapeutique le plus puissant contre les maladies mentales'. Esquirol, *Des maladies mentales* (Baillère, Paris 1838) p 398. Azoulay opened his thesis, written under the direction of Fanon, with this quote.

37 On the beginnings of Saint-Alban see Marion Rochet, 'La vie de l'hôpital psychiatrique de Saint-Alban-sur-Limagnole (Lozère) de septembre 1939 à mai 1945', unpublished Master Thesis in History, University Jean Monnet-Saint Étienne, 1993.

38 Fanon studied medicine at Lyon, where he participated in anti-colonialist demonstrations. Lyon had been the site of a trial, in 1947, the first of this kind after World War II, in which lawyers and anti-colonialists wanted to try French colonialism. The accused were colonised men from Réunion Island indicted of murder. Fanon would later say that he participated in the

demonstrations organized around this trial. At the University of Lyon he went to listen to Merleau-Ponty and André Leroi-Gouran. In 1952, he married a young French woman Marie-Josèphe (Josie) Dublé. He prepared the exam for the psychiatric hospitals with Tosquelles which he passed in June 1953.

39   Tosquelles participated to the creation of the POUM (Partido Obrero de Unificacíon Marxista), a Marxist anti-Stalinist movement created in 1935 and banned by the Republican Spanish Government dominated by the communists during the days of May 1937. He was the student of Professor Mira i Lopez, who had developed a local psychiatric institution within the cultural and political movement of 'Catalan Renaissance'. Tosquelles, who was in analysis from 1931 to 1935, became the Director of the psychiatric services of the Army of Estramadure (republican army) from 1938 to 1939. He was asked to develop and organize the psychological selection of soldiers in charge of tanks and machine guns. He escaped to France in September 1939. See Rochet, op cit; Elizabeth Roudinesco; François Tosquelles, *L'enseignement de la folie* (Privat, Toulouse 1992).

40   Spanish Republican soldiers escaping the fascist armies of Franco were put in camps by the French government. 450,000 refugees lived in the camp of Septfonds in difficult conditions. Many died of epidemics or hunger.

41   Balvet had in 1942 presented a report demanding a reform of the hospital at the Congrès des Médecins Aliénistes de Langue Française and his hospital soon attracted psychiatrists critical of the system. Lucien Bonnafé, who entered Saint-Alban in 1943, affirmed in a 1944

text that the 'recognition of the primacy of the equipment and organization will constitute the theoretical foundation upon which a veritable unity of psychiatric welfare will be built'. Cited in Tosquelles, *Éducation et Psychothérapie Institutionnelle* op cit p 45. On Bonnafé see Bertrand Foutrier op cit.

42   Tosquelles, *Éducation et Psychothérapie Institutionnelle* op cit p 34.

43   Ibid p 55.

44   *Humaniser l'hôpital psychiatrique* was the title of a collective book of essays about the experience of Saint-Alban, published in *Esprit* (vol 12 1952) and re-edited by Editions du Cerf.

45   Tosquelles, op cit p 74.

46   'Cette socialité opiniâtre et irréductible de *l'aliéné*, c'est sa planche unique de salut... Il y a là une "ouverture" thérapeutique que la médecine psychiatrique se doit d'exploiter, au maximum. Il faut croire au contresens biologique de la folie pour appréhender la folie comme erreur. Il faut parier pour *l'aliéné* contre lui-même, parier pour sa *chance* sociale contre la fatalité lamentable de son destin'. Cited in Tosquelles, op cit p 75. Emphasis in the text.

47   Georges Daumezon, 'Action individuelle de la psychothérapie collective' in *L'Évolution psychiatrique* (1952) pp 475-506. Emphasis mine.

48   On the activities of the Resistance at Saint-Alban, see Rochet pp 111-115.

49   'Le fou est celui qui est "étranger" à la société et la société décide de se débarasser de cet élément anarchique' and 'Être socialisé, c'est répondre au milieu social, accepter

que le milieu social influe sur moi'. Frantz Fanon, 'Rencontre de la société et de la psychiatrie. Notes de cours, Tunis, 1959-1960'. (Université d'Oran, Études et Recherches sur la psychologie en Algérie-CRIDSSH, n.d). The introduction says, 'The publication of these notes from a course of Frantz Fanon which Madame Bensalem had the generosity to give us offers the following interest'. This does not clarify whether Mme Bensalem, one of his students in possession of the notes who gave them to the University of Oran for publication, had in hand the notes written by Fanon for this course or if they were notes taken by her.

50   'Le colonisé est-il un être fainéant?' Fanon asked, and answered: 'La paresse du colonisé est une protection, une mesure d'autodéfense sur le plan physiologique d'abord'. ibid p 15.

51   In psychiatric hospitals, wards were segretated by sex. In the colony, a segregation by ethnic group was added to segregation by sex. Fanon was in charge of two wards: a ward with 165 European women and a ward with 220 Muslim men. Fanon had attempted to apply the principles of institutional therapy at the hospital of Pontorson Normandy in 1953, but ran into an important resistance from the administration which complained about him. A new medecin-chef was nominated. See: Claudine Razanajao and Jacques Postel, 'La vie et l'oeuvre psychiatrique de Frantz Fanon', L'Information Psychiatrique, (1975. 51:10 pp1053-1972). The issue is devoted to Fanon.

52   Jack [sic] Azoulay, 'Contribution à l'étude de la socialtherapie dans un service d'aliénés musulmans', unpublished Thesis of Medicine, University of Algiers, 1954. See also Frantz Fanon and Jacques Azoulay, 'La socialthérapie dans un service d'hommes musulmans. Difficultés méthodologiques', L'Information psychiatrique, 1954. 30:4 pp 349-361.

53   Azoulay's thesis is a fascinating and clearly written account of the evolution of Fanon's experience at Blida.

54   In a 1955 article written with J Dequeker, R Lacaton, M Micucci and F Ramee, Fanon deplored the condition of psychiatric assistance in Algeria. The authors described the lack of resources, the difficulties of recruiting trained staff, and asked for a comprehensive policy for psychiatry in Algeria. Though they congratulated the administration of Blida for its understanding and support for their experience of transforming the hospital, they concluded that their working conditions were not satisfying. 'Aspects actuels de l'assistance Mentale en Algérie', L'Information Psychiatrique (1955 31:1) pp11-18.

55   The role of the Algerian nurses in this experience has been noted in different essays. The nurse as mediator, translator, and interpreter of the culture to the non-native psychiatrist deserves a whole study. Fanon did not speak Arabic fluently and further needed an interpreter for the different languages spoken in Algeria. He began his reflections on culture and medicine as early as 1952 with his essay 'Le syndrome Nord-Africain', Esprit (February 1952) re-edited in Pour la Révolution Africaine (François Maspéro, Paris 1969 pp 9-21). English translation by Haakon Chevalier in Toward the African Revolution op cit pp 3-16. See also Frantz Fanon and François Sanchez, 'Attitude du Maghrébin

Musulman devant la folie', *Revue Pratique de Psychologie de la vie sociale et d'hygiène mentale* (vol 11956) pp 24-27 in which Fanon and Sanchez argued that in traditional societies mad people have been socially 'integrated'. This approach has been, since then, reassessed showing a more complex reality: the mad person was 'tolerated' only to be considered as a beast or as divine.

56   According to Bégué, since the opening of the European hospital, women and Muslim men had constituted the majority of its patients.

57   Jeanne Favret and Jean-Pierre Peter, 'L'animal, le fou, la mort' in *Moi, Pierre Rivière, ayant égorgé ma mère, ma soeur, et mon frère... Un cas de parricide au XIXe. siècle* (Julliard, Collection Archives, Paris 1984) pp 243-264.

58   Ibid p 254. See also Frantz Fanon, 'Colonial War and Mental Disorders', op cit; Jacques Lacan, 'Motifs du crime paranoïaque: Le crime des soeurs Papin' in *Le Minotaure* (vol 3-4 1933 pp 25-28). In this essay, Lacan analyses the crime of two sisters who, in 1933, savagely killed the woman they worked for and her daughter. The sisters had killed, according to Lacan, to destroy the ideal of the master that they had internalised. They were model servants, who had internalised the ideal of servitude.

59   See the remarks of Porot about the soldiers of the colonial armies, these 'stupid men taken from their *bled*'.

60   Fanon, *The Wretched of The Earth* op.cit. p 303. Emphasis in the text.

61   Fanon was, according to the testimonies of his friends, a very caring person: a lively, playful, curious, charismatic man with a love for friendship and parties. It is

therefore not his capacity for caring that I challenge but the ways in which he constructed decolonisation. Commandant Azzedine gives us the testimony of an encounter between Fanon and himself: 'I met Fanon in 1959 in Tunis. I was wounded. My first memory: Fanon as a psychiatrist, he feared that I was not well. He asked: "How are you? I would like to know, I know the moral demand of the Algerian struggle, but when was the last time you had sexual intercourse?" I thought, but is this his business? I was shocked. I answered him and he helped me. Now he is dead and I am alive, but he cured me'.

62   Fanon, *Black Skin, White Masks* op cit p 231. Emphasis mine. This sentence is repeated in different forms throughout Fanon's text.

63   The first day care hospitals opened in England. There were no day-care hospitals in France in 1959. See Frantz Fanon and Charles Geronimi, 'L'Hospitalisation de Jour en psychiatrie. Valeur et limites' in *La Tunisie Médicale* (1959 38:10) pp 713-732.

64   This position would later be fully developed by the antipsychiatrists.

65   'Toutefois l'aspect capital de l'Hôpital de Jour consiste dans la liberté entière qu'il laisse au malade, brisant de façon éclatante avec la coercition relative et quelquefois absolue que revêt l'enfermement'. In 'Hospitalisation de Jour,' op cit p 715.

66   Frantz Fanon, 'Fondement réciproque de la culture nationale et des luttes de libération' in *Présence Africaine* (1959:24-25) pp 82-89. The English translation is in the chapter 'On National Culture' in *The Wretched of the Earth* trans Constance Farrington, op cit p 36.

67   Ibid p 35.

68   Frantz Fanon, *The Wretched of the Earth*, op cit.

69   Gail Caldwell, 'Author Toni Morrison Discusses Her Latest Novel *Beloved*' [1987] in ed. Danille Taylor-Guthrie, *Conversations with Toni Morrison* (University Press of Missouri, Jackson 1994) pp 239-245. On 'writing slavery' see also Toni Morrison, *Playing in the Dark: Whiteness and the Literary Imagination* (Harvard University Press, Cambridge MA 1992); and of course, her novel, *Beloved* (A Plume Book, New York 1988).

70   Abraham and Torok, *L'écorce et le noyau* (Flammarim, Paris 1987) p 255.

71   Elsie B Washington, 'Talk with Toni Morrison', In *Conversations with Toni Morrison* op cit pp 234-238.

72   Michel de Certeau, 'L'opération historique' in eds. Jacques Le Goff and Pierre Nora, *Faire de l'histoire. Nouveau problèmes* (Gallimard, Paris 1974) p 34.

73   Ibid p 34.

74   Homi Bhabha, 'Freedom's Basis in the Indeterminate', *October* (vol 61 Summer 1992) pp 46-57 p56.

75   Fanon and Geronimi, 1956 op cit p 732. Psychiatry has continued to develop in 'under-developed' countries. It is regarded as a technique which best answers the needs of deprived populations. The World Health Organisation has, in a recent report, advocated an increased coordination between native healers and psychiatrists. Ethno-psychiatry has finally earned its legitimacy. About psychiatry in Algeria after independence, see Mahfound Boucebci, *Psychiatrie, Société et développement* (SNED, Algiers 1982). (Boucebci, a respected psychiatrist, was assassinated in June 1993 at Algiers); and the special issue of *L'Information psychiatrique* (vol 66 December 1990).

76   The Algerian historian Mohamed Harbi has argued that the militarisation of the struggle led to a militarisation of society, and this militarisation, to him, was among the factors that led to the actual situation in Algeria. According to Harbi, Fanon supported the partisans in the FLN of the armed struggle suspicious that negotiations would lead to unacceptable compromises.

bell hooks

Feminism as a persistent critique of history:

What's love got to do with it?

If and when woman as subject for storying or history is conceived as militant, she must be faithful to the subversive logic or graphic of plurality and thus become part of the body of all struggles.

Gayatri Spivak. Outside in the Teaching Machine: French Feminism Revisited

To open up the body of history and expose it to the vindications of the world involves the adoption of a figure of time, of knowledge, that is also a figure of speech, or writing, able to hold in suspension the ambiguous 'truth' that language sustains in our combined re-writing of the past as we research the historical potential of the present. For style is the body, the physicality of language. So, we acknowledge in the gesture of a style - of thought, of writing, of speech - the co-presence and responsibility for past, present and future.

Iain Chambers. The Baroque and the Judgement of Angels

Looking back in order to negotiate a return to the subject of 'working with Fanon'

At the outset of the Working with Fanon conference at the ICA I was disturbed by the way in which gender issues, of which a focus on sexism is only one, were, as is so often the case, relegated to the margins and seen as the concern of women thinkers and scholars. Ideally, progressive critical thinking and theory should always examine a subject from a standpoint that considers feminist analysis, what it means to do critical work in a manner that does not reinforce sexist thought and action.

Usually, when a panel of women discuss feminist approaches to a male scholar, the assumption is that the focus will be solely on interrogating his sexism. Concurrently, when women who advocate feminism are gathered together, it is usually assumed that there will be little or no dissent; that women will be supportive, protective and unified. Embedded in such thinking is the wrong-minded assumption that solidarity cannot co-exist with dissent. Of course, no one assumes that male critical thinkers gathered to speak on any subject are not intellectual comrades capable of remaining in solidarity even if they disagree. Given the way in which sexism continues to shape the way women thinkers are seen, the moment women disagree, conflict is reduced to pure spectacle. The meaning and significance of the disagreement is lost in the shuffle.

Our panel began with the moderator presuming that we would concentrate on interrogating Fanon's sexism, stating that we would not only engage in the rigorous task of working with Fanon but that we would also be 'working him over'. This metaphor immediately situated all three female speakers in an antagonistic and symbolically violent relationship to Fanon. This stance not only evoked the stereotypical assumption that a feminist standpoint is rooted in anti-male sentiment, but also made it appear as though discussing sexism was our primary agenda. Since much of the work I do within the discourse of revolutionary feminist thought focuses on issues of race, and in particular the issue of challenging sexism whilst simultaneously creating a place for feminist transformation in black life, I try to debunk the stereotypical assumption that feminist politics are rooted in anti-male sentiments and at the same time point out that such an assumption, made on a constant basis, will destroy the possibility of progressive political solidarity between black women and men. Naturally then, both as a moment of critical intervention that was meant to disrupt the imposition of the moderator's thoughts and values onto the rest of us, and to challenge this assumption from the standpoint of advancing feminist politics, I disassociated myself from the agenda that had been set and created a space of dissent. To negotiate a shift in tone, mood and intent I spoke spontaneously. I began by telling a story. I began with confession.

Reuniting that which has been broken: a remembering of improvisation

Believing both in the power and necessity of humour and play both in intellectual discourse and revolutionary struggle, I told this little story and re-tell it here. I chose it because it came directly out of my personal struggle to sustain intimacy with male comrades and loved ones. I wanted to create, in that dimly-lit theatre in which the conference was taking place, a feeling of the meaning of intimacy, the place of longing in our private lives and our public works. I wanted to talk from the spaces in my heart of longing for true love, intimacy and partnership with men in my life. (Let me pause here to say that the printed word cannot adequately convey this moment of critical intervention: the disruption I created was engendered as much by the seductive tone of my voice. Too bad no audio tape accompanies this printed page!). The story:

I want to begin by saying that I have no interest in 'working over' Fanon and that I am concerned with the issue of love both in regards to the way it informs Fanon's notions of freedom and its relation to a contemporary liberation struggle. I want to understand his declaration: 'Today, I believe in the possibility of love, that is why I endeavour to trace its imperfections'. I am interested in the issues of love between black women and men. Months ago I had a session with a psychic in which we talked about what stands in the way of love. She suggested that I had to deal with my anger towards men. While I was willing to consider the potential 'truth' of her reading, I did not agree with it. I called the men in my life I love and am closest to and asked them if they felt I was harbouring repressed rage and anger. I called my father, my brother, ex-lovers; the list went on. As I pondered her comments, I kept returning to the issue of fear. And whilst I did not see anger, I saw fear in myself. It recalled to mind lines from Amiri Baraka's poetry: 'What I thought was love in me - I find to be a thousand instances of fear'.

Recently my father has been ill. As he ages I not only contemplate the possibility of his death, I come face to face with my fear. I have lived most of my life in fear of him - of his rages and his indifference. To reach the love between us I have to come face to face with this fear and move past it to talk openly and honestly with him; to make a space for confrontation and reconciliation. I have to face my fear of losing him just when we have re-found the love between us that was there when I was a small child; when he was not afraid of me and I was not afraid of him. As Fanon says, 'Today, I believe in the possibility of love, that is why I endeavour to trace its imperfections, its perversions.' Dialogue makes love possible. I want to think critically about intellectual partnership, about the ways black women and men resist by creating a world where we can talk with one another, where we can work together.

Working with Fanon: a return to love

When I first read *The Wretched of the Earth* I heard a new history spoken - the voice of the decolonised subject raised in resistance. That voice was full of seductive passion and desire. It articulated a yearning for freedom that was so intense and a quality of emotional hunger that was so fierce that it was overwhelming. Dying into the text, I abandoned and forgot myself. The lust for freedom in those pages awakened and resurrected me. In that moment of recognition, gender had no meaning. An ecstatic moment of critical break-through always takes me out of my body. No wonder then that I was not disturbed by Fanon's patriarchal standpoint. I knew how to move through the body of the father to discover myself. In my girlhood, it had not been possible to imagine oneself as thinker/writer/interrogator without projecting oneself into the phallic imaginary; into the body of the father. Only by journeying through the body of the father could I connect with the mind.

Already a resisting reader whenever I heard the sound of my father's own voice, I knew how to let go every sound he uttered that was destined to limit and confine me as surely as I learned to cling to every word that brought me closer to a freedom that enabled me to leave my father's house - to leave home. It was the practice of being a resisting reader that enabled me to hear in Fanon's theories of decolonisation, paradigms I could use constructively in order to liberate myself. In my late teens, my struggle for liberation did not begin with imperialism, the nation or even white supremacy, despite the situation of racial apartheid in which we lived. It began with the body of the father. Nowadays I am often asked to chart a critical genealogy of my intellectual development. In the years before I became deeply engaged with the feminist movement and with the writing of feminist theorists, all the progressive critical thinkers who nurtured my emergent radical subjectivity were men: Fanon, Memmi, Cabral, Freire, Malcolm X. These men taught me to think critically about colonialism. They were my intellectual parents. In rooms in which it seemed no women were allowed to enter, they gave me ways to invent and make myself.

Fascinated by my journey through the body of the father, I forgot about mothers. The feminist movement returned me to the body of the mother. Suddenly all the knowledge I had gained from reading texts written by men in dialogue with other men were too confining. They lacked a liberatory standpoint that I found in feminism's exploration of ideas. Feminist thinking demanded that I moved beyond patriarchy, beyond the body of the father. Initially, to do this I needed to forget: to repress the father's words and be born again in the memory of the mother's body. This was an act of finding and listening to the female voice; mine, those of my female ancestors and feminist comrades in struggle.

During this process of conversion to feminist politics I often forgot my patriarchal intellectual parents. For a long time I left Fanon behind. The memory of how his work had transformed me was deeply submerged. Although I spoke proudly and affectionately of the ways works by Malcolm X, Memmi, Freire and Cabral inspired me in my books, there was little mention of Fanon. In retrospect I see in his work a profound lack of recognition of the presence of the mothering body, of the female body that thinks. It is the symbolic matricide enacted in his work that necessarily severed the connection the moment I embarked on a critical journey with feminism that began with the recovery of the mother's body.

Returning to Fanon after almost 20 years of keeping his words at a distance, I seek to find again that moment of innocence and unknowing wherein his words touched the longing for freedom within my female body, and called me into that continuous state of mental revolution: where strategies of resistance can be imagined, where theories of liberation must be endlessly invented and reinvented to speak directly to the lived experience of the moment. These strategies of resistance must speak to, with, and against a vision of history that remains unrealised, that is all too limited and narrow to be fully liberatory. As Fanon stated, 'Was my freedom not given to me then to build the world of the *You*? At the conclusion of this study, I want the world to recognize, with me, the open door of every consciousness. My final prayer: O my body, make me always a man who questions!' Often the body that makes us question, that makes us interrogate reality anew, is the body that is in the process of breaking down. Recently, when I re-read *The Wretched of the Earth* I heard the sound of the father speaking and I recognised for the first time Fanon's insight that the body of the father was a body in pain, a body awaiting loss, a body longing to be re-membered.

Fundamentally, Fanon's writing is concerned with issues of healing. Often he situates that concern within a discursive framework that deflects it, making the primal insight one which suggests that the mind needs to be well in order to be vigilantly engaged in a liberatory process or, as the slaves in the south used to say, 'stayed on freedom'. To be well, the mind would need to question, as the descendants of those same slaves did when they sang these lyrics: 'is it well with your soul, are you free and made whole?'

Throughout *The Wretched of the Earth* Fanon offers paradigms for the healing of the dispossessed, colonised black body politic. Within this dialectic he writes gender through race. The blackness/darkness of the colonised body that marks it as other to the white coloniser is always framed within a gendered context wherein the metaphors of emasculation and castration symbolically articulate the psychic wounds of the colonised. That pain then is inscribed always as the pain of men inflicted upon them by other men. Healing, as Fanon envisions it, takes place only as this conflict between men is resolved. The fact of colour as it impacts on the well-being of women and men is eclipsed in a paradigm of healing that suggests all will be well when men are able to reach a level of homophilia: a quality of love for one and another that precludes the possibility of domination and dehumanisation so central to the maintenance of the coloniser/colonised relationship. I first thought of Fanon's writing on the bonds between men in this gendered script as homosocial. Then Paul Gilroy suggested the term homophilia would be more appropriate because it not only highlights love of men for men but, more profoundly, 'love of the same'. This distinction is crucial to understanding Fanon, since the male bonding he evokes as necessary for the project of progressive cultural and political revolution is not an essentialised patriarchal brotherhood between all men irrespective of their differences: it is the bonding of a select group of enlightened intellectual men, linked by a shared vision. Hence his insistence; 'The problem is to get to know that place that these men mean to give their people, the kind of social relations that they decide to set up, and the conception they have of the future of humanity. It is this that counts; everything else is mystification, signifying nothing.' However much Fanon speaks about a 'corporeal schema', the body is continually subordinated to the mind and will of enlightened men, whose freedom, as he envisions, necessitates privileging the mind as that space of transcendence where ultimately the body and its skin colour can be forgotten.

In order to subordinate the corporeal world to that of the mind, the mother's body must disappear along with the body of the father so that a world of fraternal sameness and brotherhood can emerge. To establish a fraternal order, a brotherhood of men - organised to further their mutual benefit and to attain common goals - critical dialogue among men is necessary, as is the recognition of shared subjectivity. The presence of the female disrupts the possibility of this unmediated bonding. In Fanon's case, remembering the mother requires a return not only to the black body but to the black female body. Symbolic matricide allows for the erasure of that body so that the fraternal paradigm can be posited as the site of hope and possibility. In this world without others, the idea and presence of the father also loses significance and meaning.

Fanon is not seeking to recover a world of absent black fathers or present white fathers. Indeed, he posits a world where biological bonds must be negated in the interest of creating a new liberatory world order grounded solely in a shared vision. Biology is never destiny for Fanon. To repudiate biology one must not seek healing via an exploration of a critical psychic genealogy that demands an examination of one's past. Fanon feels 'nausea' when confronted with a corporeal schema that demands that he be 'responsible at the same time for my body, for my race, for my ancestors'. This turn from the past makes fixation on the bonds between coloniser and colonised the only site of struggle. Hence, he can never turn his gaze away from the face of the white male other. It is this perversion that leads to the construction of a paradigm where blackness can only be understood in relation to whiteness. To fulfil the demands of such a paradigm it is essential to erase the female.

When Fanon declares that 'the black person has no ontological resistance to the white gaze' he denies that the interaction between black males and black females might serve as just such a site. But he could not have arrived at this insight without surrendering his fascination with homophilia. It is precisely the mutual patriarchal gazing - the competition for the status of 'real' man - that creates the blind spot in the liberatory analysis of those white and black men who cannot see 'the female' and thus cannot theorise an inclusive vision of freedom. The sado-masochistic crux of the Hegelian master/slave dialectic is ruptured when the black female is recognised as an 'other' with whom the black male may, in acts of solidarity, engage in various states of ontological resistance.

To consider relations between black females and males as a possible site of resistance one must first critique the reduction of female identity to the world of the corporeal. Fanon never engages in this critique. Not only is the female body, black or white, always a sexualised body, always not the body that 'thinks', but it also appears to be a body that never longs for freedom. Radical subjectivity as Fanon conceives of it is registered in the recognition of that longing to be free. This desire is seen only as present in the hearts of men. Reciprocal recognition, then, is always about men desiring men. It is a love affair between black men and white men. That Fanon consciously writes this desire through a gendered narrative caught up in a process of consistent desexualisation is rooted in his denial of the female presence.

The Fanon of *The Wretched of the Earth* is not unaware of the place of women in the struggle. Now and then he evokes a world of universal humanism where women and men are struggling. This is usually when he is speaking of Algeria and rarely when he is speaking of dark-skinned Africa. In that world the site of struggle is always between men. He refuses to recognise the presence of the female because it would require a surrender of the fraternal bond. Calculated refusal has to do with the absence of desire. His desire is not towards the incorporation of a progressive dialectic of revolution that would demand the creation of a world where women and men in general, and black women and men in particular, would dialogue together. Undoubtedly, this refusal on Fanon's part to shift his gaze - away from men, away from black men, and towards a vision of reality that would acknowledge the presence of women in struggle, especially the presence of black females - is linked to his refusal to see any value in interrogating the individual's personal past. It is here that his paradigms for healing fall short. He succumbs to that very 'lack of imagination of the heart' that he so powerfully critiques.

To claim the space of care and love that is necessary for the psychic healing of wounds inflicted not only by the dysfunctions created by racism but by the myriad dysfunctions rooted in traumas experienced in our families of origin, there must be a willingness to explore the links between the two experiences. It is these links that Fanon represses and suppresses. Indeed, if we, as black people, internalise the belief that we have no ontological resistance to the white gaze, then we can never imagine a world where complex critical investigation of the bonds between black people are deemed not only worthy of study but necessary to any full 'reading' of our psyches and our histories.

Working with Fanon's writing in the formative stages of my political development, I was given by this intellectual parent paradigms that enabled me to understand the many ways in which systems of domination damage the colonised. More than any other thinker, he provided me with a model for insurgent black intellectual life that has shaped my work. He taught me the importance of vigilant interrogation. Certainly I took him at his word when he passionately declared. 'Was my freedom not given to me then in order to build the world of the *You*? At the conclusion of this study, I want the world to recognise, with me, the open door of every consciousness. My final prayer: O my body, make me always a man who questions!' In becoming a woman who questions, I found feminist thinking transformed my understanding of the work of Fanon. I returned to him through my embrace of both mother and father; through a recognition of their mutual presence within me. It is a return to love. Looking back, looking critically, I now see in the body of Fanon's *The Wretched of the Earth* the longing for that return.

Lola Young

Missing persons:

Fantasising black women in
Black Skin, White Masks

The following consists of a reading of Frantz Fanon's *Black Skin, White Masks* which privileges gender, referring particularly to the terms in which women are discussed in the text. I will argue that black and white women are inscribed differently in *Black Skin, White Masks* and that in Fanon's writing there is evidence of a deep seam of fear and rage regarding black women. My aim is not, as it may at times appear, to deny the contribution which Fanon makes to a discussion of the psychological effects of colonialism and racism, but to draw attention to the ways in which he has constructed pathological models of the psychosexuality of women.

As Henry Louis Gates Jr points out in his essay 'Critical Fanonism', 'Frantz Fanon has now been reinstated as a global theorist' and this bestows upon his work on 'race', gender, sex, colonialism and psychoanalysis a particular authority.[1] It is this authority, at the conjuncture of 'race' and gender, that I wish to problematise.

I want to start with a quite basic issue, one raised briefly by Homi Bhabha in his introduction to the 1986 Pluto Press edition of *Black Skin, White Masks*, one which is, I feel of crucial importance: when is 'man' not a man, but people? According to Bhabha's note at the end of his essay, Fanon's use of the term 'man', 'connotes a phenomenological quality of humanness inclusive of man and woman'.[2] However, this usage is never entirely stable. Sometimes that 'man' means 'Frantz Fanon', sometimes 'black man' and sometimes 'human being'. This is not simply a question of tracking down the sexist use of a generic pronoun, it is a matter of the ontological status of black women. Those who have little or no power are so categorised not just because they have nothing but because they are nothing; they are excluded because they are considered to be nothing. Are black women in or out of the frame in Fanon's statement which begins 'The black is a black man...'? In or out of the frame when Fanon asks, 'What does a black man want?'[3]

Fanon's men

Fanon responds to his question with the statement that 'The black man wants to be white'[4]. Fanon's men have complex lives and experiences of the world, and the language he uses to describe and analyse this world is powerfully evocative. Fragments of bodies and minds are metaphorically strewn about the text in order to represent the feelings of alienation and fragmentation of the psyche, and the encounter between black and white men is marked, to use Bhabha's words, as an 'objectifying confrontation with otherness'.[5] In a lengthy footnote (and it is worth reflecting on those instances where Fanon makes significant comments about black masculinity and confines his observations to footnotes), Fanon invokes Lacan's mirror phase and elaborates on this 'confrontation'. The struggle between black and white is to be conducted on a 'man to man' basis:

> When one has grasped the mechanism described by Lacan, one can have no further doubt that the real Other for the white man is and will continue to be the black man. And conversely.[6]

The unassimilable 'body-image' based both on an 'epidermal schema' and possession of the phallus renders white and black women - on one level - peripheral to the central contest. Further examination demonstrates that black and white women are accorded differentiated textual status, since although the motivations of both come under his scrutiny, Fanon's uneasiness in thinking about the specificity of black women's experiences of racism and colonialism is palpable.

Black woman no cry?

For his analysis of black women's attitudes, desires and shortcomings, Fanon is mainly dependant on the autobiographical account of Mayotte Capécia in *Je Suis Martiniquaise*.[7] Fanon represents this 'mulatto' woman as particularly problematic since she is seen as participating in racial suicide through her attempt to engage in a sexual relationship with a white man. Referring to the reactions of 'the woman of colour' - who he represents as either the 'Negress' or the 'mulatto' - to white European men, Fanon writes:

> The first has only one possibility and concern: to turn white. The second wants not only to turn white but also to avoid slipping back. What indeed could be more illogical than a mulatto woman's acceptance of a Negro husband? For it must be understood once and for all that it is a question of saving the race.[8]

Thus he maps out the black woman's burden.

Why does Fanon select three largely fictionalised accounts - one of which is written by a man - to extrapolate theories on black women and their relations with white men? Indeed he cannot justify such a strategy, and later admits:

> there was a touch of fraud in trying to deduce from the behavior of Nini and Mayotte Capécia a general law of the behavior of the black woman with the white man... [9]

Mayotte Capècia
Je Suis Martiniquaise
Editions Corrêa, Paris (1948)

This confession only emerges in his later discussion of Jean Veneuse, the black man with whom a white woman is in love: this is after the vitriol of Fanon's account of black women has settled. Of course, it may be argued that what we are confronted with here - as in Fanon's later assertions about white women - is a writing style comprised of generalisation and hyperbole in order to provoke. But what is Fanon masking - and foregrounding - through this textual strategy?

Fanon's unforgiving analysis of Capécia begins with her narrative of childhood attempts to 'blacken' the world by tipping ink over a white boy's head. Fanon is keen to develop a sense of Capécia's unconscious, even without access to her dreams:

> ... since she could no longer try to blacken, to negrify the world, she was going to try, in her own body and in her own mind to bleach it.[10]

The latter point refers to what was to become her job of washing people's clothes. This psychoanalytic explanation for her 'choice' of occupation as a laundress ignores the gendered division of labour and the options available to black women for achieving economic independence. Fanon refers to her laundering as a displacement activity for her desire for whiteness, or in his terms, as a desire for 'lactification'[11]. This is a suggestive term when considered alongside his use of the figure of the 'black mother' in the text, a point to which I shall return briefly later. Fanon assures us that the necessity to 'whiten the race' is something that 'every woman in Martinique' knows and allegedly acts upon:

> It is always essential to avoid falling back into the pit of niggerhood, and every woman in the Antilles, whether in a casual flirtation or in a serious affair, is determined to select the least black of the men.[12]

There is nothing here about the colour choices of black men in the Antilles. The specificity of black women's experiences lies in their attempts to annihilate the 'black race' through 'lactification', and in their perpetuation of a colour/caste system which serves the interests of the coloniser.

This assessment of the 'woman of colour' must also be considered in the context of the racial identities assigned to the women cited in this chapter: they are all 'mulattos'. Fanon's assertions then imply that the essential quality of the 'mixed race' or 'mulatta' female is her desire not to slip back into 'niggerhood'. Fanon's anxiety about the racial identity of the eponymous heroine of *Nini* - a fictional text which constitutes another piece of his evidence on black women's behaviour - is expressed in his over-elaboration of her identity: she is at once a 'mulatto', 'She is almost white' and 'a girl of color'. She is the emblematic 'mulatto' woman: 'Nini', 'Nana', 'Nenette'.

If 'race' is an ontological symbol, how does the 'mulatto' fit into or disrupt the power of racial categories? These 'almost white' subjects - and Fanon refers mainly to women - are figures that embody racial liminality, occupying the interstices between the terms black and white, Negro and Caucasian, other and self. Thus, the 'mulatto' subject disrupts the normalisation of the divide between blackness and whiteness.

The novel *Nini* by Abdoulaye Sadji (a black male writer) is discussed by Fanon as though it were an unmediated depiction of essential black femininity.[13] Fanon states that: 'She [Nini] was no longer the woman who wanted to be white; she was white. She was joining the white world.'[14] If this is compared to other accounts of women who 'pass' for white - for example, in Nella Larsen's *Passing* - the issues which arise from the attempts to assume an unproblematic whiteness, are for women of colour, often literally life-threatening. Fanon gives no sense of a feeling for, or interest in, the reasons and consequences for adopting such strategies.

There is a class issue here too: Mayotte Capécia aspires to move up in the social as well as the racial hierarchy through her relationship with a white officer, a gentleman. Whilst Capécia is a mere washerwoman, Nini, who is pursued by Mactar (a black man who 'had the gall to write to her') is referred to as a 'stupid little stenographer.'[15]

Fanon collapses Mayotte Capécia's *Je Suis Martiniquaise*, Abdoulaye Sadji's *Nini*, and Paul Morand's *Magie Noire* into each other. 'The same process is to be observed' he claims, concluding that 'It is because the Negress feels inferior that she aspires to win admittance into the white world.'[16] Fanon then goes on to pathologise this Negress by diagnosing her as suffering from 'affective erethism'.[17] Contrary to Jock McCulloch's assertion that, 'Affective erethism is the term Fanon uses to describe the massive sensitivity of the Negro', this term is applied only to the 'Negress'.[18]

Fanon only refers to black women's experiences in terms which mark her as the betrayer (tainted with white blood). He even goes so far as to juxtapose the author of virulently racist tracts, Count Joseph Arthur de Gobineau (who wrote the four volume text *Essay on the Inequality of the Human Races* in 1854) with Mayotte Capécia: 'I am thinking impartially of men like Gobineau or women like Mayotte Capécia', an indication of his antipathy to this and other similar 'women of colour'.[19]

The sense of black women's problematic presence, and frequent absence as significant beings, is consolidated when Fanon reiterates his ambivalence to black women through what may be regarded as a re-working of Freud's 'dark continent' trope. Of his experience of black women's pyschosexuality, Fanon confesses 'I know nothing about her'.[20] Consider also Fanon's oft quoted passage in the chapter 'The Fact of Blackness', which begins:

> "Mama, see the Negro! I'm frightened!" Frightened! Frightened! Now they were beginning to be afraid of me... [21]

In this scene, which depicts the playing out of the struggle between black men and white men (the boy as 'white man-to-be'), there is the coming together of the white boy, the white mother and the objectified black man. The missing person in this 'race'/gender configuration is the black female. How might this sequence work with a different cast of characters? What if the scene were of a white father and daughter, with the child gazing at a black woman? Would the little girl speak out in public in the same startling manner as the little boy? In this new scenario, might not the father have initiated the sequence of looks, being male, being white? Would the black woman quiver with fear and self-loathing? Might she not, in any case, be invisible? Fanon does not speak of the fantasies and images of black women which may inform white men's perceptions of black female sexuality, a fact that is consistent with his textual rather than experiential encounters. Since the power implicated in the act of looking and being looked at is asymmetrically allocated to white and black, to male and female, in racially stratified patriarchal societies, changing the sex of the participants in this ritualised version of the encounter between black and white to one which focuses on a black woman as the object of the look, serves to foreground a different set of relations and experiences: a set of relations upon which Fanon does not turn his own critical gaze.

Black men are not held to be responsible - as black women are - for the 'denegrification' of the 'race' because they do not bear children. In Fanon's terms, 'mulatto women of color' threaten the stability of the racial order both by the capacity of their visible presence to undermine the difference between black and white and by their choice of white male partners. Black women are then, more of a threat to black survival than white men, and the anxiety which they generate is exacerbated by their unknowability.

Black men: Jean Veneuse/Frantz Fanon

It is important to note the terms which Fanon uses in 'The Man of Color and the White Woman', in comparison to those used in 'The Woman of Color and the White Man'. Significantly, here Fanon imbues inter-racial sex with political motivation as well as the desire to be white. It is about the attempt to 'grasp white civilization and dignity and make them mine.'[22]

Whereas the 'woman of color' with white antecedents is locked into the debilitating prison of self-inferiorisation and inappropriate aspirations, Fanon's black man has no trace of 'white blood' to mar the purity of his identity. Jean Veneuse reads philosophical and literary texts, is introverted and a sentimentalist. This is in stark contrast to belittling, narcissistic women such as Capécia and Nini, described as 'All those frantic women of color...'[23] with 'their need to gesticulate, their love of ridiculous ostentation, their calculated, theatrical, revolting attitudes.'[24]

Fanon grants Jean Veneuse a universalist notion of humanity which he denies black women:

> Jean Veneuse is the crusader of the inner life... Jean Veneuse is a neurotic, and his color is only an attempt to explain his psychic structure. If this objective difference had not existed, he would have manufactured it out of nothing.[25]

And unlike other Antillean men who journey to France, Veneuse can resist a desire for white women. Whilst for many:

> ... the dominant concern among those arriving in France was to go to bed with a white woman... once this ritual of initiation into 'authentic' manhood had been fulfilled, they took their train for Paris.[26]

Thus black male sexual acts with white women constitute an initiation, a black male rite/right of passage into masculinity - conquering and debasing the white man's possession - rather than simply a betrayal of the race.

Black women initiate relationships with white men, indeed they strategise and then stalk their prey, whereas Jean Veneuse is the 'lamb to the slaughter' with whom women attempt to flirt.[27] He loves his one, specific white woman, whereas the women of colour want any white man who can enhance their racial, economic and social status. Veneuse writes poetry; Capécia is imbecilic.[28]

White women's whiteness

For Fanon, sex for the black woman is about effacing blackness and gaining power and wealth, whereas for white women it is sexual experience with the phobic object which is desired.

Fanon claims that sexual frustration is the principal constituent of white women's anxieties about black people, marking them as inherently prone to sexual neurosis, and locating racism as an effect of their frustration. His statement about white women's racism and its alleged link with their lack of a sexual life again appears overstated:

> All the Negrophobic women I have known had abnormal sex lives. Their husbands had left them; or they were widows and they were afraid to find substitutes for the dead husband; or they were divorced and they had doubts at the thought of a new object investment.[29]

However, together with other allusions to white women's desires and fantasies, *Black Skin, White Masks* does at least suggest a concern with the inner world of white women's psyche which is again in contrast to the lack of engagement with black women's psyches. He also refers to white women who have a more substantial existence than that of a character in a novel.

Fanon notes the remarks of a white girl who expresses her terror of black men which sets out for him the various stages of negrophobia.[30] (Note that these comments are located in the context of speculation regarding male homosexual rape and an implied link between homosexuality and racism):

> Basically, does this fear of rape not itself cry out for rape? - Just as there are faces that asked to be slapped, can one not speak of women who ask to be raped?[31]

Fanon's later analysis of white female sexual desire should be noted here too. He posits that:

> The fantasy of rape by a Negro is a variation of... 'I wish the Negro would rip me open'.[32]

Are fear and desire so indissolubly linked? So Fanon claims. Or is it that desire may be masked by fear, especially where the desire is prohibited, and to fulfil it would be an act of transgression?

Fanon feels able to unravel the enigma of the Negrophobic white woman by locating her behaviour in the desire to have - and be raped by - a black man. Fanon sees this psychosexual positioning as being analogous to the Negrophobic white male's repressed desire for a homosexual relationship with a black man. Thus, 'The white man is sealed in his whiteness' but not completely in his heterosexuality. This casual allusion to homosexuality and negrophobia is disturbing since it not only psychopathologises racism but, by linking the two together, marks homosexuality as a 'white man's disease'. This is an assertion that Fanon links to the alleged absence of the Oedipal complex in the Antilles. However, it might be useful to think through what may be characterised as Fanon's apparent hatred and fear of the 'feminine' here, and what that might mean in terms of the repression of his own desires.

Mothers and sons

White women as well as black women are generally positioned as the repository of the 'race' (exemplified in the frequency of the question 'would you let your daughter marry a black man?'). Both are expected to support the values and traditions of the patriarchal order but are also seen as the weak links in the effort of sustaining racial integrity. Thus white women's neurotic instability means that they may regress from culture to nature. This is suggested by Fanon's account of the waking dream of a white woman undergoing therapy: she plays on the slippery terrain between civilisation and savagery fantasising that, ' "She danced around the fire and let the Negroes take her hands." '[33] Meanwhile, black women 'emasculate' and render black men 'impotent' (sexually and politically) by their desire to be white.

The figure of the black mother is occasionally included but only to be castigated as the root of dysfunctional behaviour in her sons. So that, for example:

> When I am at home my mother sings me French love songs in which there is never a word about Negroes. When I disobey, when I make too much noise, I am told to 'stop acting like a nigger.'[34]

In her role as custodian of the culture the maternal black woman fails to provide the support required and this dissatisfaction with the mother is embedded in, and explained by, Fanon's statement that he does want to be loved because of a bad previous experience where he was eventually abandoned. This 'mother' may also be a figure for Martinique and Africa, and represent the rage engendered by the sense of abandonment by the mother country.

Women are emphatically actual or potential child-bearers in Fanon's script. In his narrative, to rework Hortense Spillers' phrase, the term daughter, 'drops out of' Fanon's 'critical protocol':

> ... the patriarchal daughter remains suspended as a social positionality between already-established territories... bearing a name that she carries by courtesy to legal fiction and bound toward one that she must acquire in order 'to have' her own children, 'daughter' maintains status only insofar as she succeeds in disappearing, in deconstructing into 'wife' and 'mother' of *his* children.[35]

Perhaps this too is part of Fanon's rage, for Capécia, Nini and the others may be read as resisting the powerlessness embedded in their situation by refusing to participate in the ritual exchange of women as prescribed within the community.

Endnotes

At the beginning of 'Critical Fanonism', Henry Louis Gates Jr quotes from *Black Skin, White Masks*: 'This book, it is hoped, will be a mirror'.[36] The extent to which this works for black women is questionable. I have indicated that this mirror is held up for men to gaze into whilst women look on: if the women are black, then they pause to look only at the white man, awaiting his confirmation of their desirability, and the opportunity to have their blackness consumed by his whiteness; if they are white, gripped by a neurotic negrophobia fuelled by sexual frustration, the women hesitate whilst they consider whether to indulge their fantasies of rape by black men.

White women may be seen to have an oscillating status which means they can be self and other to white men: they are white but not male. The black man serves as both an anchor to weigh down and stabilise white male identity, and a potential competitor for white women's affections.

Unfortunately, the black woman, being neither white nor male, represents a double lack in the psycho-sexual colonial schema: the antithesis of both whiteness and established notions of femininity and masculinity. In addition, for the black male who aspires to patriarchal

Sonia Boyce
Untitled (1995)
Colour laser print
on vinyl. 16' x 14'
Sonia Boyce

power, the black woman represents an encumbrance. Is she chained to the white woman in the same way that white and black males are bound together? Jock McCulloch's reading of Fanon claims that the '*imago* of the Negro is a convenient means by which the white woman retains her psychic balance' and thus the white woman has the black woman for her other.[37] In this model then, the black woman desires but is not the object of desire since she has no status to confer on those who might want her: on this basis, she is written out of the scenario. She serves as the other of others without sufficient status to have an other of her own.

In *Black Skin, White Masks* black woman's subordinate position is confirmed by the use of the generic he/Negro for all but the most specific of instances relating to women which are clearly marked as 'Negress'. This is the only time we can be sure that black women are included.

Fanon's resonant last words in *Black Skin, White Masks* are 'My final prayer: O my body, make of me always a man who questions!': it seems to be the case that black women cannot take it for granted that such a role within black politics and culture will be recognised without struggle.

1   Henry Louis Gates, 'Critical Fanonism' in Critical Inquiry vol 17 no. 3 Spring 1991 p 457.

2   Homi Bhabha, 'Remembering Fanon', foreword to Frantz Fanon, *Black Skin, White Masks* (Pluto Press, London1986) p. xxvi.

3   Frantz Fanon, ibid p 10.

4   Frantz Fanon, ibid p 11.

5   Homi Bhabha, op cit p. xvii.

6   Frantz Fanon, op cit p 161.

7   Mayotte Capècia, *Je Suis Martinquaise* (Corréa, Paris 1948), as quoted in Frantz Fanon, ibid p 42.

8   Frantz Fanon, op cit p 54.

9   Frantz Fanon, ibid p 81.

10 Frantz Fanon, ibid p 45.

11 Frantz Fanon, ibid p 48.

12 Frantz Fanon, ibid p 46.

13 Frantz Fanon, ibid p 53.

14 Frantz Fanon, ibid p 58.

15 Frantz Fanon, ibid p 55.

16 Frantz Fanon, ibid p 59.

17 Frantz Fanon, ibid p 60.

18 Jock McCulloch, *Black Soul, White Atrifact: Fanon's Psychology and Social Theory* (Cambridge University Press, Cambridge 1983).

19 Frantz Fanon, op cit p 12.

20 Frantz Fanon, ibid p 180.

21 Frantz Fanon, ibid pp 112-114.

22 Frantz Fanon, ibid p 63.

23 Frantz Fanon, ibid p 49.

24 Frantz Fanon, ibid p 57, quoting Sadji.

25 Frantz Fanon, ibid p 78.

26 Frantz Fanon, ibid p 72.

27 Frantz Fanon, ibid p 66.

28 Frantz Fanon, ibid p 52, footnote 12.

29 Frantz Fanon, ibid p 158.

30 Frantz Fanon, ibid p 151.

31 Frantz Fanon, ibid p 156.

32 Frantz Fanon, ibid p 179.

33 Frantz Fanon, ibid p 207, quoting notes on Mlle B, a patient admitted to the psychiatric hospital of Saint-Ylie.

34 Frantz Fanon, ibid p 191.

35 Hortense Spillers, '"The Permanent Obliquity of an In(pha)llibly Straight": In the Time of the Daughters and the Fathers' in ed. C A Wall, *Changing Our Own Words: Essays on Criticism, Theory and Writing by Black Women* (Routledge, London 1990) pp 127-149.

36 Henry Louis Gates, 'Critical Fanonism' op cit p 457.

37 Jock McCulloch, *Black Soul, White Atrifact: Fanon's Psychology and Social Theory* op cit p 74.

Dialogue

Lola Young
bell hooks
Gilane Tawadros
Martina Attille
Mark Latamie
Homi K Bhabha
Françoise Vergès

Tawadros I'd like to start with Fanon's many fantasies and desires. I'd like to ask Lola Young a question about the particular chapter in *Black Skin, White Masks*: 'The Woman of Colour and the White Man'. Is there, in the dismissal of Mayotte Capécia's narrative, which Fanon at one point calls a 'narrative of corruption', a trace of Fanon's own desires for the purity of the race, for blackness to be experienced as a state of wholeness?

Young Of what might the text be symptomatic? It is difficult to resist the idea of it being possible to read Fanon's desire through the book. With regard to racial integrity, it seems to be something Fanon sees might be possible or present through men rather than through women. There is a sense of a tainting of blackness with whiteness that he picks up with regard to Mayotte Capécia as well as fictional characters within the chapter.

Tawadros Fanon seems to be unable to perceive the relationship between a woman of colour and a white man in any terms other than her desire for whiteness, and for there ever to be anything but an echo of the master/slave relationship within that black/white relationship.

Young More troubling is the absence of the black woman and the black man as attractive figures. Other unspoken relationships are alluded to in the footnote about homosexuality. Another missing relationship is that between black women, not necessarily within a sexual framework but simply as friends.

Tawadros bell, how can the missing intellectual relationships be mapped?

hooks I try to map it in a different way, without evoking female powerlessness and lack of agency. In my paper for the conference I began by naming my own agency in claiming a relationship with Fanon, a fact that enabled me to be nurtured and grow through work despite sexism. I am trying precisely not to fall back into this kind of binary that assumes that if there is a sexist or patriarchal standpoint, then there's no way to enter the text. I was trying to enter the text in terms of my own capacity to utilise the discourse around colonialism. In a sense, I was trying to make myself appear in the text, to find a space, to talk about what I take to meet the way Fanon makes the black female disappear; to negotiate.

One of the images being used a lot in US advertising campaigns at the moment is the black male body on his knees to a white female. What strikes me is the narcissism of the fact that neither of them are looking at one another. To think about who is the absent figure that is being gazed at takes us back to that trope of homophilia, the relationship to the white male, to the longing for the sense of the white male as representing the only meaningful father towards whom one looks for recognition. Fanon cannot get to himself without going back in some way through the body of the father, the black father, who is equally a disappeared person within the narrative. So it is not wholly a question of the disappearance of the female. In some ways, it is a disappearance of the question of home. I think that one of the things that we might think about is the juxtaposition of home and nation. The current narrative of nation is very distinct from a narrative of home, of origin, that would in fact require us to think both in a personal and a collective way about our relationship to black mothers and fathers - those relationships that are equally disappeared.

Tawadros   I can't help reading something rather romantic in what you are invoking here.

hooks   I think I'm deeply romantic. Do you mean in a way that suggests frivolousness or utopianism?

Tawadros   Not frivolous but utopian. I cannot disengage *The Wretched of the Earth* as a narrative from a reading of a colonial struggle from which women were not absent but were very much present. The very disturbing and horrific descriptions of the traumatised bodies in that book are the bodies of men. Women appear in those texts as victims of a secondary trauma, after the colonial trauma. The reason I found it difficult to read that through your mapping is that I find, at this particular historical moment, that a kind of separatist struggle, which articulates itself against the grain of colonialism and postcolonialism, persists in setting women out of that frame, even where they have been active in the first stages of that struggle.

hooks   You are telling a story that interests you. It interests me too, but it's not the story that I wanted to tell today. These are not competing narratives. To have a radical feminist deconstruction of Fanon is not a competing narrative to the one that I propose, but a stage in the development of my own thinking. One need not cancel out the other. It was precisely that discourse on colonialism that, in the early stages of feminism, gave us a sense of complete erasure. One of the things I realised in re-reading *The Wretched of the Earth* was how profound a crisis African-Americans find themselves in right now. There's a certain wretchedness in our lives. We are at another point in history in which our people are facing a concrete crisis and are deeply divided within the realm of gender. I said that gender is being written though the trope of race: that there is a gendered narrative that needs to be looked at not as a secondary narrative to the narrative of race and Fanon and any other thinkers that we might talk about, but actually as a potential competing narrative that subsumes and superimposes itself in a certain kind of way.

Young   Here you say that there's a sense of those narratives competing, whereas in a slightly different context earlier you said that is wasn't necessary for them to compete.

hooks   I'm talking about two different stories. One is about a radical feminist deconstruction and the other is a radical feminist vision of the potential future. I see, in particular psychoanalytically, that if the longing for recognition is always for recognition by what we might call the white father as the only possible world, then that gendered narrative always competes with any attempts to envision a future. What will decolonisation mean for us after the revolution? Is there any point in even imagining what happens beyond that if in fact our gaze cannot be shifted? That's why I see it as a narrative that keeps Fanon and many of us locked down because we cannot move within it.

Young   Where is the basis of constructing the politics of solidarity that you were talking about earlier?

hooks   In love. I was thinking a lot about the place of empathy in any kind of ethic of care and the notion that part of how one embraces that larger you - that you that Fanon uses - is through the capacity to embrace the other in some way. What does it mean if Fanon is unable to embrace the black female - what part of himself remains unembraced? How does the possibility of love or an ethic of care chart the path to this humanism that he poses as redemptive?

Tawadros   But surely that's the contradiction at the heart of that particular chapter in *Black Skin, White Masks*, because Fanon cannot conceptualise a relationship that could be based on the desire for difference rather than the desire for sameness. I think that may relate to what you were saying about homophilia. He starts by saying man is 'motion toward the world and toward his like'. For me this is a contradiction: the impossibility of the desire for otherness. It can only be the desire to be the same.

hooks   That's because the only bond I think that interested him is the homophilic one. In my own writing I say 'Dying into the text, I abandoned and forgot myself'. It's useful for me to think of Fanon dying into this sado-masochistic bond with the male/white other where all things cease. But all things do not have to cease because they are not interesting or compelling, they cease because they don't interest *you*. They cease because when you enter that space with the one you love, you don't see anything else. I'm not disagreeing with you, but that is to me the point that I want to critique and interrogate. I'm not trying to apologise for that, or for the violence that is enacted in the name of that bonding.

Attille I must say that Fanon's *Black Skin, White Masks* is a fantastic object to work with. Within a modern context he offers a possibility to read between the lines, and as an artist and film-maker myself, I do this as an insider. Some of the models he sets up (especially black man/white woman, white man/black woman) allow me to draw on my experience - to draw on the complexities of those relationships and the secrets that are not disclosed within his text. Mayotte Capécia's work, *Je suis Martiniquaise*, is not available in English and is thus, tragically, encased in Fanon's work in a derogatory way. Because when I read Fanon's quotation of her text I recognised the black woman and something of what was going on in the desire for this white man, I could see how aspects of that desire were also about Capécia's own narcissism. I managed to track down some pages from the text on microfiche in France. There is one scene where she is in the bedroom with the white man. She's awake before him and she sits on the edge of the bed with her back to him, fantasising about him without even looking at him. At another moment in the text she looks at her best female friend Loulouze and feels something that she can't quite articulate.

The idea for my work, *The Smile*, which used Capécia's text on the mirror in the ICA bar as part of *Mirage*, opened a path for thinking about misunderstandings that have occurred much closer to home than across the black/white divide or the male/female divide. It also created the possibility of looking much closer at the people around my immediate space at the same time as generating an anxiety at doing that. For me to read between the lines of Fanon I first of all make connections within my own family and the fantasies of my own family members about what might happen to them in the future, by prying through their personal belongings, and reinventing their family albums. Then I create another symbolic level where I can deal with the subject. Fanon is exciting because my private experience and personal vernacular enable me to imagine the complexities and the violence.

Martina Attille
Smile #2 (1995)
Text from Mayotte Capécia
Je Suis Martiniquaise,
Editions Corrêa, Paris (1948)
Image: Musa Bananier,
from *Histoire Naturelle,*
Botanique (Marechal)
Natural History Museum
Picture Library, London

Ma mère suspendait devant ma bouche
un régime de bananes. Je cherchais
alors à les attraper, car je les adorais.
Je crois bien que c'est par gourmandise
que j'ai appris à marcher.

Les mouvements de Loulouze me
causaient une sorte d'émotion. Parfois
aussi, elle se baignait avec nous. Elle
avait une peau dorée qui tenait de
l'orange et de la banane, de longs
cheveux noirs qu'elle roulait en tresses
et qui m'étaient crépus qu'à la base, un
nez assez épaté et des lèvres épaisses,
mais le visage d'une forme telle qu'elle
devait avoir des blancs assez proches
dans son ascendance.

What frightens me is that the academy doesn't allow for a clear integration of the private and the public in such an intimate agenda.

Tawadros To that extent would you agree with bell hooks that there is a possibility to inscribe yourself within the text, that you can create that space?

Attille I don't think Fanon allows me to do that directly. I think it was that quote from Mayotte Capécia that allowed me to recognise a way of looking, a way of deluding myself and a way of wanting to be desired and recognising desire of the other for me as a way of becoming desirable. What Lola Young says about the desire of a black woman conferring no status on the desired is interesting to me. What Fanon does is give me some insight into the dynamics of the rage that exists between black men and black women.

Latamie The problem you have raised is in fact a particular problem in Martinique. Nobody talks about it. We have a white society that controls the economic relation with France. Fanon was born in this context and he never raised the point directly. I think all the problems he explored in his work came from that story. The feminist side is very complicated to clarify, but I have one suggestion: there were rarely relations between black men and white women in Martinique but white men did have relations with black women. Martinique was and still is a very matriarchal place. The mother is the head of the family; she runs the family and raises the kids and makes the economic life of the family possible. The father is never present. Fanon could not bring this subject up.

hooks I was thinking about how much the logic of black male/female symbolic relations as they appear in the absences and the gaps in Fanon's texts - the obvious situatedness of black woman as betrayer of the race - informs a cultural agenda that is both within the realm of cultural nationalism and outside that realm as well. To what extent does the black male body find itself unable to stake out a terrain for itself within whiteness that does not necessitate the erasure of female bodies in such a way that there can be no 'imagination of the heart', to use Fanon's phrase; where one cannot even think about a politics of solidarity? Black people have been able to imagine a politics of solidarity within a cultural nationalist framework. The question becomes what kind of solidarities do we then talk about specifically between black men and women in a context of a narrative of freedom that is not rooted in nationalism, but that is rooted in universal humanism (a term with which I am comfortable). That politics of solidarity can never be arrived at if we are not able to grapple with the question of gender not as a side issue, but as central to the heart of the matter. Which is why I would insist on a calculated refusal: certainly we have to situate *The Wretched of the Earth* within the historical moment taking place globally for women and therefore cannot see Fanon mired in this innocent sexism where he constructs a gendered narrative without an understanding of the tensions and conflicts, but we also need to see that he does so for a purpose.

Bhabha   In this context, I was wondering what you would think about Fanon's refusal of Oedipal anxiety within the Martinican family? This seems to me on the one hand to be a fairly radical concept - to relativise the Oedipus complex, to say 'you cannot use this as a universal narrative'. However, if you actually by-pass something like that anxiety, then do you also write out the figure of the mother or the question of gender-differentiation as a moment that has to be negotiated? This is not to say that the Oedipal narrative is empowering to women - I'm not making any such claim - but I do think something happens when we appreciate that Fanon wanted to relativise by producing a sociology. But can you get rid of Oedipal anxiety sociologically?

hooks   It is not a question of whether *Oedipal* anxiety exits but whether *anxiety* exits. Fanon could have rearticulated that anxiety on a whole different level specific to the cultural context. But in his effort to win in a discourse with the West, he had a need to negate that question of influence rather than articulate anxieties. This goes back to the whole concept of purity. At moments he attempts to win out over the white person. That's why he doesn't spend his time trying to name for us the dynamics in that family context.

Young   There is a tension between wanting to reconcile the use of psychoanalytical theory and trying to insert race into the discourse of psychoanalysis. If there wasn't this Oedipal moment in Martinique, what was there? As bell hooks says, what produces the anxiety? And what are the kinds of consequences that one could think about as a result of that kind of initiation into sexual difference - what would that mean about the way people think, for example, about their sexuality?

Tawadros   In the specific context of anti-colonialist struggle, the position of women and modernisation, the demands to modernise and to liberate women have become and are becoming inscribed with a complicity with colonialism; a complicity with Westernisation and modernisation that I see reccurring. In the Middle East right now, the assault of neo-colonialism is resisted by reverting to a kind of solidarity which at the same time disempowers women yet again. So the women who once removed veils in the street and were at the vanguard of a national struggle are now watching as another generation literally mask themselves again.

hooks That's why we have to be willing to conceptualise another type of solidarity. If we don't, then people in times of crisis will fall back on already charted maps of solidarity that are linked to nationalisms and fundamentalisms. We can see that in the USA right now. Fanon is accountable for that failure as well as many other male figures who have been our visionaries in so many other ways. It is precisely to work with the point where they stop that allows us to go forward.

Gilane Tawadros Words like 'solidarity' and 'universal humanism' are loaded. What is this solidarity? You have to begin to name it.

hooks I think many of us feel that we are in the process of naming it.

Vergès It seems to me that the mother is nonetheless evoked in *Black Skin, White Masks*; the mother who, for instance, forbids the little boy to sing Martinican songs, who sings French songs to him and, when he wants her to sing Martinican songs, says 'don't play the Negro here'. What I think is totally absent is the father, as Mark Latamie has said. This is related to the question of the primal scene of slavery where the father remains passive of the rape of the black mother by the white man. Fanon does not know what to do with this scene. Where is the father who is going to protect his son and save his woman from rape? The figure of the woman is one that betrays, even if this betrayal is caused by a rape of which she is the victim. Fanon is haunted by that, and the text is haunted by the question of rape and the fear of rape, and the black male body fearing rape - rape by the white homosexual man or by the white woman.

Young I have been thinking about the double paternity of the black father and the white father. The figure of the father is a painful figure which can be said to re-evoke those memories around slavery and what they mean in terms of the construction, deconstruction and destruction of the black family.

hooks In *The Wretched of the Earth* there is a quality of nostalgia linked to how Fanon comes home. When he comes to the imaginary home in the imaginary nation, the black male/white male bond is countered with the evocation of an African nation that these men would build. When I used the terms 'father' and 'mother' I used them in a re-articulated sense. When Fanon talks about what men will do, so many of the terms he uses are those we would normally associate with an idea of the feminine; a sense of nurture, a sense of care, a sense of giving. That's one way to think about loss, and why *The Wretched of the Earth* is framed in the way it is: a heart-to-heart dialogue from one black man to other black men with white men looking on in envy. The envy of a certain quality of ecstasy leaves you behind and goes on to affirm itself somewhere else.

Kobena Mercer

**Decolonisation and
Disappointment:**

Reading Fanon's Sexual Politics

Drawing out some of the themes from the essay I contributed to the *Mirage* exhibition catalogue, I would like to pick up on three strands of the conference debate[1]. The first relates to the interrogative character of the dialogue between the legacy of Fanon's ideas and the concerns diaspora artists have with issues of postcolonial subjectivity. In relation to this I would like to highlight questions of gender and sexuality as indicative of a significant, generational, shift. The second theme relates to the questions with which Stuart Hall starts this book: why Fanon, why now, and why *Black Skin, White Masks* in particular? In response to these questions my comments seek to situate a contemporary re-reading of Fanon in relation to sexual politics as the Achilles heel of black liberation. My sense is that questions of sexuality have come to mark the interior limits of decolonisation, where the utopian project of liberation has come to grief. The third theme is about the changing historical relationship between psychoanalysis and politics, and the question of locating the violence: where the violence comes from and where it goes.

Amongst diaspora artists of the 1980s and 90s, the interest in *Black Skin, White Masks,* in contrast to Fanon's other texts such as *The Wretched of the Earth, Towards the African Revolution* or *For a Dying Colonialism,* could be understood as a response to the failures of revolutionary nationalism - the political failure of the radical humanist utopian vision associated with Fanon's name in the past. It is, however, important to have the opportunity to re-assess criteria of success and failure, for although a concern with collective memory has been a major theme for contemporary black British artists, there is also a widespread understanding that many of us would probably not even be here were it not for the nationalist revolutions and anti-colonial struggles of the 1940s, 50s and 60s. Moreover, given the hybrid location of diaspora artists in the West, it is important to recognise that, as well as the attempt to make sense of what was not delivered by the Third World revolutions of the past, there is also an attempt to come to terms with the legacies of Freud and Marx in relation to the social movements of the metropolis.

The sociological term 'new social movements' may seem to suggest that political movements around race, gender and sexuality are fairly parochial even though they have been around since the Enlightenment and are probably not going to go away. It is this ideological intransigence that diaspora artists have sought to address in their work. Across a range of activities undertaken by visual artists and practitioners in live arts and cinema, all of whom contribute to various forms of postconceptual art, it could be said that a key marker of generational differences has been a dual engagement with the theoretical narratives of Marxism and psychoanalysis in relation to postcolonial cultural practice. Perhaps one could localise this generational narrative quite narrowly, in the British context, in terms of the legacies of the film studies journal *Screen* on the one hand, and the Centre for Contemporary Cultural Studies on the other. In contrast to earlier interpretations of Fanon that were influenced by, say, pan-Africanism and existentialism, contemporary readings have been mediated more by the shifts associated with Althusserian and Gramscian approaches to ideology and the Lacanian approach to subjectivity.

By characterising diaspora art practices as postconceptual, I mean not only to imply that contemporary artists refuse the dichotomy between theory and practice, but that what diaspora aesthetics have placed in the foreground is an actively dialogic relationship with the conceptual frameworks and problematics that postcolonial theorists have delineated, most often in relation to literary texts. Issues of ambivalence, fetishism, paranoia and masquerade have been investigated by artists in their own right. I raise the issue in this way because it is somewhat mistaken to assume that visual art is theory-led. Visual artists are exploring diverse forms of knowledge that are not necessarily identical to that which gets produced in rational, analytical, discourse. Questions which Lyle Ashton Harris raises later in this volume about a certain resistance to the aesthetic experience of the work itself, and which Renée Green raises by signalling the risk that art may even be reduced to the illustration of theoretical insights, strike me as important aspects of what is interesting about this dialogue, but which also indicate what is difficult about the way that interpretative authority is often invested in theory *per se*.

Once we set the hybrid formation of diaspora aesthetics into the black Atlantic context that is shared by artists in Britain and the United States, one can see the articulation of inquiry into issues of ambivalence, fetishism and paranoia as a point of departure for interventions in a cultural war of position. This is about winning popular identifications to radical democratic values. For example, with regard to cinema and the proliferation of black film-making over the last ten years, one might say that the exposition of what a postnationalist subject position might look like has not only cleared space for the recognition of diversity and difference within and between the ethnic identities that make up the imagined unity of the nation, but has offered an alternative to the resurgence of neonationalism. Whilst both neonationalism and postnationalism could be said to recognise the ending of black nationalism's narrative of cultural unity - 'one aim, one people, one destiny' - the former seeks a nostalgic and conservative way of shoring up a monolithic conception of group identity, whereas the latter offers the alternative of confronting the experience of loss and uncertainty in order to examine what political potential resides in what was repressed in earlier historical narratives of national identity.

This is something that can be seen at work in the late 1980s black British independent sector in films such as *Dreaming Rivers* (Martina Attille, 1988), *Twilight City* (Reece Auguiste, 1989), *Testament* (John Akomfrah, 1989) and *Looking for Langston* (Isaac Julien, 1988). The films were each archaeological in orientation, exploring what had been hidden from history in order to dig up resources for imagining the present differently. But another interesting feature, which few critics picked up, was that all of the films were about mourning. They are about the loss of a loved object; whether this was a parent, an artistic figure, a city, or a political ideal. Similarly, this commitment to the work of mourning can be seen in fine art installation such as *A Ship Called Jesus* (1991) by Keith Piper, which manifests an interesting synchronicity alongside Paul Gilroy's examination of the technology of the ship in the history of the Atlantic triangle.[2] Piper tackles the loss of political certainty not with nostalgia but with a refusal to flinch from the difficult ambivalence in the diasporic imaginary - especially in its religious and biblical forms of expression - whereby the conservation of radical values of memory and community may fuel both a progressive politics of liberation and a conservative politics of retribution.

Zarina Bhimji is another visual artist who has consistently explored the darker side of postcolonial subjectivity. Right from early image-text work such as *She Loves to Breathe... Pure Silence* (1987), there has been a subtle evocation of innocence and violation which suggests that her work is not about identity, but how subjectivity is constituted by otherness and, above all, by trauma. Informed by feminist scepticism over figurative representation, which constantly risks re-fetishising the image of the female body, Bhimji's installation *I Will Always Be Here* (1992) uses objects such as burnt kurta shirts to uncover the unrepresentable losses out of which fragile identities emerge through language and symbolisation.

Finally, film work such as *The Attendant* (1993) and *The Darker Side of Black* (1994) by Isaac Julien, again manifests this commitment to difficulty; a commitment which is actually a modernist virtue, and not something one readily associates with populist varieties of postmodernism. Developing from earlier works that consistently locate the point of critical intervention at the intersection of sexual divisions and social fantasy, the films involve a recognition of sexuality as a point of access to complexity - in the sense that eros arises from chaos. In contrast to what some might see as the 'celebration' of black sexuality in films like Spike Lee's *She's Gotta Have It* (1986) or *Mo' Better Blues* (1990), a postnationalist location recognises sexuality as that which constantly worries and troubles anything as supposedly fixed as an identity. Whilst it may be implausible to describe the aesthetic practices of each of these artists as Fanonian in any direct or didactic sense, I think their key concerns with displacing the former certainties of the nationalist narrative can be said to converge within a dialogic space in which contemporary re-readings of *Black Skin, White Masks* have taken place.

I want, then, to discuss the way such cultural practices draw our attention to sexual politics as the interior limit of decolonisation. This means holding on to the emancipatory vision which Fanon theorised in terms of liberating the subjectivity of coloniser and colonised from an oppressive symbolic universe, while at the same time acknowledging the disappointment consequent upon the loss of such a utopian vision in the face of the relentless rightward political shifts of the past ten to fifteen years.

We realised towards the end of the 1980s that, although the centre/margin metaphor was useful to describe the bewildering changes associated with postmodernity, it was also inadequate because it retained the notion of society as a closed entity, as opposed to, say, Ernesto Laclau's idea that the social is a dislocated structure with multiple centres of power and resistance.[3] Nevertheless, when one takes account of the way black lesbian and gay cultural practitioners have been at the forefront of decentring former narratives of national identity, the metaphor retains its validity in describing forms of social agency responsible for the demarginalisation of postcolonial subjectivities. One might even find in this context a lovingly perverse parody of DuBois' rather elitist notion of the 'talented tenth', especially in the light of the right's current campaign to get our presence in the body politic reduced from 10% - Kinsey's consensual post-war statistic - to something like 1%.

Marlon Riggs' *Tongues Untied* (1989) offers a key moment in which what might seem relatively marginal work by black gay artists has been at the very centre of the political turmoil manifested in the 1990s culture wars. As the first of its kind - a coming-out film for black gay men - *Tongues Untied* had to negotiate the politics of representation inherent in being the 'first' film to do this, which it did quite eloquently, unpacking its burden of representation in order to expand the space for other black gay and lesbian film-makers. This is neither a minoritarian, particularist nor exclusivist claim I am putting forward regarding the interest and importance of the film. Rather it is a political claim that concerns the universalist character of the ethical questions raised by new social movements, which was measured by the response of audiences for the film who were neither black nor gay, nor remotely interested in expanding the chain of democratic equivalencies in order to express solidarity with us. I am thinking of right-wing fundamentalists in the US like Pat Buchanan, who is cut from the same cloth as Rush Limbaugh, another media-literate public figure who has come to embody the angry, straight, white, male identity now leading the backlash against the relative success of the '1980s radical democratic movements.

In his bid for the 1992 US presidency Pat Buchanan appropriated a clip from *Tongues Untied* to argue that George Bush, via the National Endowment for the Arts and the Public Broadcasting Service, was squandering tax-payer's money on what the wretched right are nowadays happy to call 'victim art'. The most interesting feature of the campaign advert was not that it required the disavowal of the fact that black queer citizens pay their taxes too, nor that it attempted to refuel the moral panic around obscenity initiated by Senator Jesse Helms over Robert Mapplethorpe's photographs. Rather, the most bizarre aspect of its representational logic was that it did not show any images of black gay people at all. There is a brief segment in *Tongues Untied* depicting white leather-queens in San Francisco's Folsom Street fair, which is intended to suggest the absence of black participation in the predominantly white 'gay community'. By ripping it out of context, Buchanan's act of de-appropriation sought to construct black gay art as a national obscenity. Obscene means off-scene, and like a director of a horror film, Buchanan was clearly aware that what you do not see can be all the more horrific, all the more compelling, precisely because you do not see it.[4]

There is also another underlying reason for the editing strategy, which brings us to the question of how and why homophobia has become a key issue for black politics. Although the paranoid logic of new right demonology implies that a combination of gayness and blackness increases the otherness of the phobic object, Buchanan's decision not to depict black gay bodies may be understood as a strategic bid not to alienate potential black support for neoconservative positions. Indeed, it may be said that a culturally conservative stance on issues of sexuality and gender politics has been instrumental in winning over black participation to the new right project. On this view, one can see the sexual politics of, say, Minister Farrakhan and the Nation of Islam as a ghostly photographic negative of the embattled, siege-mentality that drives the fundamentalist offensive against liberal and radical democratic values.

Further manifestations of homophobia in black popular culture, such as ragga star Buju Banton's 1992 hit, 'Boom bye bye ina de batty man head', confront us with the key enigmas of the post-Civil Rights predicament. Can you imagine Stevie Wonder or Bob Marley coming up with a lyric like that? What has happened over the last thirty years such that a counter-hegemonic vision of universal liberation has given way to a horrific mirror-image of the politics of resentment and retribution? To the extent that such sources of disappointment are an enigma, for which there is no available explanation or narrative, perhaps this is because such issues are simply not talked about as widely as they need to be. Could it be that such silences in black politics have been perpetuated as a defensive reaction against the racialist construct that somehow blacks are intrinsically more homophobic by virtue of being supposedly closer to nature and hence 'less civilised'? It is in relation to such questions in the psycho-politics of sex and race that Fanon returns as an indispensable resource for contemporary thinking. At the risk of simplification, I would argue that one of the reasons why *Black Skin, White Masks* has been re-read with such a sense of urgency has to do with Fanon's recognition of the value of psychoanalysis as the site of the talking cure.

Psychoanalysis understands the self to be a precarious and fragile thing which is rarely the master of its own house - the id or 'it' out of which 'I' emerges. Hence, its concept of a decentred subject questions conventional notions of culpability and causality. Homophobia, in my view, must be understood in such terms because when its expression crops up in black intellectual discourses, as well as vernacular culture, we are dealing not with the platitudinous certainties of fingerpointing someone as a 'bad person,' but rather we face the more complex task of understanding how the repressed returns through the means of repression in the form of a symptom. That a leading African-American literary critic, Houston Baker, in the context of a response to the film *Looking for Langston*, rejoins an important public debate on black popular culture with the disclaimer, 'I am not gay, but...' (which is a rather unfunny parody of the disavowal implicit in the commonplace epithet 'I am not racist, but...'), strikes me as symptomatic of the way in which all that was hitherto silenced, unsaid and unspoken in the black liberation narrative nonetheless speaks volumes about the black cultural unconscious.[5]

I take responsibility for raising this as a political, not a moral, issue because I think that our survival depends on being able to bring the symptom to the site of the talking cure. I do, however, feel that this is not the way to meet and greet as we travel through what Audre Lorde, in her mythobiography, *Zami: A New Spelling of My Name*, called, 'the multiple houses of difference.'[6] The acknowledgement of differences among and between diasporic subjects cannot take place according to a binary division between me and not-me. In my view, you do not have to go there. One further point about Audre Lorde's emphasis on living with differences is the sense in which her inflection of the concept of recognition serves to question the liberal humanist idea of tolerance, which itself implies that the otherness of the other person is assumed to be intolerable. In contrast to a certain code of compulsory sentimentality, which implies that in order to recognise me you either need to be like me or that you are obliged to like me, Lorde's emphasis on the *difficulty of recognition* allows for separateness within interdependence because it assumes that the identity of the ego is neither fixed nor omnipotent. In place of the master/slave dialectic of the sovereign self, it implies an ethics that begins with awareness of the always incomplete character of a self that can alter the story of who it was before.

In bringing the counter-universalism of social movements back into the conversation, I would also like to take up Gloria Anzaldua's notion that queer coloured people are go-betweens and translators in that, 'being the supreme crossers of cultures... our role is... to transfer ideas and information from one culture to another.'[7] While this may sound to some like an essentialist claim, I take the contrary view that it helps to explain why lesbian and gay artists and activists have been in the forefront of decentring the outmoded notion of the essential black subject. A keen commitment to the aesthetics and politics of hybridity has arisen from subject positions that are highly sceptical of the binary code of gender apartheid. This is not to suggest that lesbians and gays are not implicated in the gender divide, but that homosexuals tend to get bored with either/or frontiers and hence are constantly moving between positions of masculinity and femininity in order to get out from under their apparent fixity. To the extent that what results is a denaturalisation of gender identity, everyone gets to benefit and hence queer cultural border-crossings have universalist implications for sexual equality.

It is from this standpoint that I would prioritise the re-readings of Fanon put forward by lesbian and gay cultural theorists such as Jonathan Dollimore, Lee Edelman, Diana Fuss and Darieck Scott.[8] Whilst acknowledging the insights of Fanon's analysis of colonial psycho-sexuality, each also problematises the pervasive presence of homophobia in *Black Skin, White Masks*. As Lola Young demonstrates very clearly through her close reading of misogyny in the text, Fanon's sexual politics are deeply problematic. Regarding sexual equality as a reasonable, desirable and necessary goal for black liberation, and indeed everybody's decolonisation, it could be said that Fanon missed the last train from suffragette city. He just didn't get it.

The railway metaphor can be extended: according to Lacan, the train pulls into the station and the little boy says, 'Look, we've arrived at Ladies!' and his sister replies, 'Idiot! Can't you see we're at Gentlemen.'[9] For all the apparent confusion between the one and the other, sexual difference is like a sign because it is arbitrary and conventional. The little diagram showing the doors of the toilets implies that its function is more or less identical for both genders, which is to say that the law of what Lacan calls 'urinary segregation' flows not from nature but from culture and the symbolic construction of differences. As Gayle Rubin pointed out long ago in her article 'Thinking Sex', men and women are quite similar biologically, and actually have more in common with each other than they do with a palm tree or a bicycle.[10]

Far from being an immutable anatomical fact, sexual difference becomes meaningful - all too meaningful - in transforming the little human animal into a speaking subject and a social actor precisely because of its formative status as a sign constantly implicated in rules of differentiation. If sexual difference is arbitrary and conventional, the question becomes: can gender relations be changed and are they amenable to historical contingency? Or, alternatively, how and why do they get to be repeated and what produces such fixity?

This was the starting point for Juliet Mitchell's *Psychoanalysis and*

Feminism, which I mention for two reasons. The first is that, as an index of the feminist materialist turn to psychoanalysis, it emerged in a moment of both advance and retreat among the social movements. I see a potential analogy here between the highly productive cultural politics of the mid-1970s, in which artists such as Mary Kelly and Laura Mulvey opened up new horizons of complexity, and the period of the late-eighties in which black British artists sought to renew a critical aesthetics in relation to issues of subjectivity in the politics of 'race' and representation. In both instances we can see artistic movements flourish in diacritical counterpoint to an inhospitable political climate. However, my worry is whether the earlier embrace of Lacan as absolute master - which underpinned the way *Screen*, for example, came to embody its intellectual authority as a disciplinary super-ego - might come to be repeated in certain tendencies of postcolonial criticism that seem to construct Fanon as a black Lacan, for want of a better term.[11] Thus, my second concern is about a potential retreat into theory as a result of political uncertainties in our current moment. This retreat may stem from what could be seen as the disavowal of the way in which postcolonial theory in the 1980s developed, in part, out of an anaclitic relationship characterised by 'leaning on' feminism's move towards psychoanalysis in the 1970s. The price that is paid for such disavowal is to overlook the close proximity between Fanon's most powerful insights into colonial psycho-sexuality and the violent reinscription of homophobic and misogynistic positions that repeat the worst fantasies of the black nationalist narrative.

Chapter six of *Black Skin, White Masks*, 'The Negro and Psychopathology', reveals sexuality as an anchoring point for the reproduction of relations of oppression, not only between coloniser and colonised, but among the colonised themselves. Yet it is in the context of Fanon's rigorous analysis of the libidinal economy of negrophobia that we see the return of homophobia as a punctuating term of closure in the psychiatric vocabulary of pathology that he invokes to describe the dualistic mechanisms of the colonial psyche:

> Fault, guilt, refusal of guilt, paranoia - one is back in homosexual territory... Good-Evil, Beauty-Ugliness, White-Black: such are the characteristic pairings of the phenomenon that... we shall call "manicheism delirium."[12]

Even if we acknowledge that sexual politics have been a blindspot in the contemporary re-reading of Fanon, how has postcolonial theory been able to overlook footnote 44 on page 180? I quote the passage in full in order to suggest that homosexuality is a powerful source of anxiety within Fanon's theorising:

> Let me observe at once that I had no opportunity to establish the overt presence of homosexuality in Martinique. This must be viewed as the result of the absence of the Oedipus complex in the Antilles. The schema of homosexuality is well enough known. We should not overlook, however, the existence of what are called there 'men dressed like women' or 'god-mothers'. Generally they wear shirts and skirts. But I am convinced that they lead normal sex lives. They can take a punch like any 'he-man' and they are not impervious to the allures of women - fish and vegetable merchants. In Europe, on the other hand, I have known several Martinicans who became homosexuals, always passive. But this was by no means a neurotic homosexuality: For them it was a means of livelihood, as pimping is for others.[13]

The contradictory logic of this footnote - which initially suggests that Fanon knows little about homosexuality, but which then reveals that he knows all too much - can be taken as a symptom of homophobic fixation and disavowal in the political economy of masculinity in black liberationist discourse. Once women have been excluded from positions of power and authority, the problem of the phallus - who owns it, who lacks it - nevertheless remains an issue for homosocial institutions, such as the revolutionary party or the nation-state. The either/or logic of castration is thus brought to bear on relations between men via the binary fixations of a me/not-me boundary that positions the figure of the homosexual as the enemy within. Hence, Eldridge Cleaver's punitive attacks on James Baldwin, for example, during the 1960s Black Power era.

While Fanon showed us how the paranoid-schizoid mechanisms of splitting and denial operate in the 'manicheism delirium [sic]' of colonial racism - across the banal oppositions that construct the black body as phobic object - I think that it would be rather surprising if this binary code did not somehow feature in black people's experience of the emotional reality of the unconscious. We too have our fears and fantasies that have been shaped by the violence of history.

Sometimes it seems that anything we do not want to deal with we call white. This may be trivial - 'Why are you listening to those records?', 'Why are you wearing those trousers?' - but it also reveals our share in

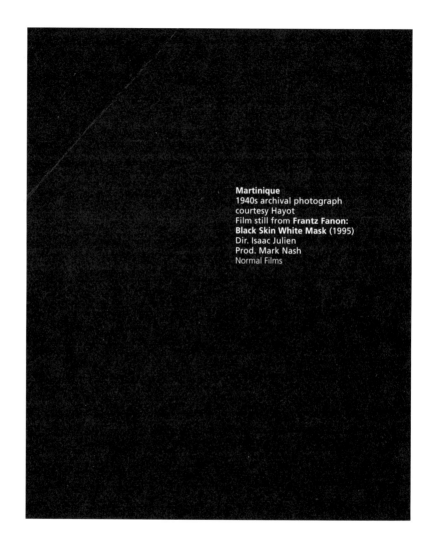

Martinique
1940s archival photograph
courtesy Hayot
Film still from **Frantz Fanon:**
Black Skin White Mask (1995)
Dir. Isaac Julien
Prod. Mark Nash
Normal Films

the universal human capacity for unpleasantness: 'Why are you sleeping with that person?', 'Why is that person having your babies?'. Something similar occurs in relation to homosexuality: 'it's a white thing'. This attitude, as a product of projection, merely expels onto the other what is deemed to be unacceptable to the ego of an authentically black identity. Homosexuality is a key issue in black sexual politics: Salman Rushdie once talked about the many rooms of literature and Edward Said has invoked the many rooms in the house of culture; I would add that the closet is one of the most crowded rooms in the house of black diaspora culture. There must be a riot going on in there! If we are to do the right thing, maybe the gesture is to let them out.

I want to end on the issue of translation. Lesbian and gay critics have reaffirmed a commitment to working with Fanon by using his analysis of negrophobia to open up the issue of homophobia both in Fanon's own text and in broader narratives of nationalism as a whole. By framing the political task of theory as one of translation there is a critical displacement of the demon of analogy among the social movements, which postpones understanding the intersectionality of psychic and social differentiation. There is also a displacement of the reductionist notion of 'internalised oppression,' a concept central to the psychological discourses that informed the project of black liberation, but one which was never filled out intellectually: the inner world remained an empty place. Moreover, while lesbian and gay presence has altered the public face of black politics, along with black feminisms in all their plurality, I would argue that the conception of sexual difference in various psychoanalytical narratives offers an alternative to the ideological traps in which an identity politics of gender can often get stuck.

Homophobia and misogyny have arisen as urgent, interlocking, symptoms of the crisis of community in an era of neoconservative hegemony. They are both psycho-sexual mechanisms that seek to secure forms of male bonding in the face of the political disaggregation of blackness in the post-Civil Rights era. Yet by falling back on coercive defences, which clearly put the compulsion back into compulsory heterosexuality, we see the repetition of a culture of retribution. This is a no-win situation for everyone - witness the escalating rates of suicide and homicide among young black men.

Once we see self and other not as two opposites that are externally defined but as interdependent locations on a möbius strip of desire and identification, we come back to Fanon's profoundly disturbing insight that coloniser and colonised mutually constitute each other's identity. However, aware that such power relations are constantly being cut across by masculinity and femininity, as arbitrary names for complex bundles of psycho-sexual positionings, we also recognise that the violence of the colonial relationship does not respect the ego's boundaries of inside and outside. In the sense that what violence does is violate the fragile boundaries established by relations of differentiation, then it has no one origin or endpoint: it has no necessary belonging. While the post in postcolonialism may often seem like wishful thinking in its implication that the unending horrors of neo-colonialism have finally passed, changes in our understanding of history, for former colonised and coloniser alike, also shift the relationship between psychoanalysis and politics. Discussing the politics of aggression in the work of Melanie Klein, in the related context of contemporary reflection on neonationalism in the Gulf War, Jacqueline Rose has drawn attention to these shifts when she argues that:

> Instead of the unconscious as the site of emancipatory pleasures, we find something negative, unavailable for celebration or release. One could argue that it has been too easy to politicise psychoanalysis as long as the structuring opposition has been situated between an over-controlling, self-deluded ego and the disruptive force of desire; that this opposition has veiled the more difficult antagonism between super-ego and unconscious, where what is hidden is aggression as much as sexuality, and the agent of repression is as ferocious as what it is trying to control.[14]

The psychoanalytic proposition that the human subject is basically constituted in division is undoubtedly pessimistic, but there is also an element of hope to be found in contemporary reworkings of Fanon's legacy in that they testify to a struggle to bring the political unconscious to the site of the talking cure: an interminable struggle to live with the thing that thinks.

Lyle Ashton Harris
Construct # 10 (1989)
black & white silver
mural print 6 x 3'
Lyle Ashton Harris / Jack
Tilton Gallery, New York

1 Kobena Mercer, 'Busy in the Ruins of Wretched Phantasia' in *Mirage: Enigmas of Race, Difference and Desire* (Institute of Contemporary Arts/Institute of International Visual Arts, London 1995) pp 15-55.

2 See Paul Gilroy, *The Black Atlantic: Modernity and Double Consciousness* (Verso, London 1993).

3 Ernesto Laclau, *New Reflections on the Revolutions of Our Time* (Verso, London 1990).

4 For an account of Buchanan's political appropriation of *Tongues Untied*, see the television programme *Over the Rainbow*, part two, 'Culture Wars' (directed by Tina Defeliciano and Jane Wagner, series editor Isaac Julien, Testing the Limits Collective, USA 1995).

5 See Houston A Baker, 'You Cain't Trus' It: Experts Witnessing in the Case of Rap' in ed. Gina Dent *Black Popular Culture* (Bay Press, Seattle 1992) p 132. See also Henry Louis Gates, 'The Black Man's Burden' ibid.

6 Audre Lorde, *Zami: A New Spelling of My Name* (Crossings Press, Trumansburg NY 1982). On the ethics of difference see Audre Lorde, *Sister Outsider: Essays and Speeches* (Crossings Press, Trumansburg NY 1984).

7 Gloria Anzaldua, *Borderlands/La Frontera* (Aunt Lute, San Francisco 1987) pp 84-85.

8 See Jonathan Dollimore, *Sexual Dissidence: Augustine to Wilde, Freud to Foucault* (Oxford University Press, New York and London 1991); Lee Edelman, 'The Part for the (W)Hole: Baldwin, Homophobia and the Fantasmatics of "Race"' in *Homographesis: Essays on Gay Literary and Cultural Theory* (Routledge, New York and London 1994); Diana Fuss, 'Interior Colonies: Frantz Fanon and the Politics of Identification' in *diacritics* vol 24 nos. 2-3 1994; Darieck Scott, 'Jungle Fever? Black Gay Identity Politics, White Dick and the Utopian Bedroom' in *GLQ* vol 1 no 3 1994.

9 Jacques Lacan, 'The agency of the letter in the unconscious or reason since Freud' in *Ecrits: A Selection* (Tavistock, London 1977) pp 151-2.

10 Gayle Rubin, 'Thinking Sex: Notes for a Radical Theory of the Politics of Sexuality' (1982) in ed. Carol S Vance *Pleasure and Danger: Exploring Female Sexuality* (Pandora Press, London 1989).

11 An issue raised in an important survey of postcolonial theory by Henry Louis Gates; 'Critical Fanonism' in *Critical Inquiry* vol 17 no 3 (University of Chicago, Chicago 1991).

12 Frantz Fanon, *Black Skin, White Masks* (Grove Press, New York 1967) p183.

13 Frantz Fanon, *Black Skin, White Masks* ibid p 180.

14 Jacqueline Rose, 'Negativity in the work of Melanie Klein' in *Why War?* (Blackwell, Oxford 1994) pp 143-4.

Dialogue

Homi K Bhabha
Françoise Vergès
Kobena Mercer
bell hooks
Isaac Julien
Members of the audience

Bhabha   In Fanon, does the issue of resisting mourning and melancholia also appear in the construction of masculinity as a defence against that form of difference that Kobena Mercer has mentioned: the defence against homosexuality? Is there a link between these two issues?

Vergès   The male body is extraordinarily present in *Black Skin, White Masks,* as is the question of rape. Rape is central to Fanon's fear of attack on the black male body. It seems to me that, because of this, the couple he invokes is mother/son. The black father is absent - the father working in the fields and on the sugar plantation. Against and because of this absence, Fanon tried to construct an international fraternity of men, a union of brothers. What he called a 'new humanism' was contained within an ideal of international fraternity - which, in the 1950s, had its radical dimension.

Mercer   I was interested in the way the question was framed. The prosaic alternative to melancholia is depression. Clinically, in terms of statistics, depression is identified as a women's mental health disorder. Obviously we know that sexual difference is not absolute, but there is a relationship that Freud establishes between melancholia and femininity which has to do with the turning inwards of the drive. If one thinks about it in relation to depressive anxiety, the question could be about homophobia as the denial and disavowal of difference *vis-à-vis* femininity - femininity as it is lived on the inside of masculine psychic structures.

Bhabha   I agree with Kobena Mercer, but I also want to establish that this is a disavowal of memory; an inability to think difference within an ambivalent structure. In Freud's *Mourning and Melancholia* ambivalence persists: the object is both present and absent. You cannot stop the mourning and you cannot just cease the melancholia. The object is both inside and outside; its temporality is the fascinating engine or motor of the whole process. This is why the Freudian notion of splitting is important in Fanon. He says 'I was split in three'. But interestingly, he immediately rushes to sociologise that moment. He does not allow space for the whole question of desire with which we associate the issue of splitting.

Mercer   It is also just as well to bear in mind that when we are talking about the father and mother - present and absent - we are also talking about representations. But I agree that the hasty sociologisation, however important it is in terms of relativising universalist claims that the psychoanalytical institution has made, allows us to lose sight of the fact that we are talking about psychic representation. The father is always the dead father. It is always a signifier in his place - the phallus - that helps organise sexual difference within the patriarchy. I think that recognising the specificity of representation is important.

Bhabha   This then becomes a real problem for the politics of Fanon. Françoise Vergès had made me feel a bit depressed - even melancholic - about the lack of access to the symbolic in Fanon. This means that the splitting into three can never actually lead to a 'further'; we do not have the option that, for instance, French feminism offered in saying that we can be *jouissant*, eternally orgasmic, post-colonial. There is also a resistance to mourning. So there is a type of 'presentism' in Fanon.

Vergès   But if we are to work with his ghost then we have to acknowledge the other ghosts that, although he tried to bury them, nonetheless move through the text.

Audience   Françoise Vergès, could you explain a little more about the distinction Fanon makes between history and biography? Why is history a positive force for him, and what did he mean by that? Why does biography represent amnesia?

Vergès   Fanon thought that you had to be 'active' in history which, to him, meant that you had to 'force' history. In *Black Skin, White Masks* he often quotes Pierre Naville who was then trying to marry psychoanalysis to a Marxist understanding of history. But whereas you can choose your own history - in the sense that you can make it - you cannot choose your own biography. You can re-invent and re-imagine biography, but then it will be just that: and invention; a fictional family romance in which imagined parents are always better - wealthier, more heroic, strong - than your real parents. Fanon worried about the complexities of desire, the conscious and unconscious contradictions revealed by individual narratives. He feared that they could constitute obstacles to decolonisation. For him, decolonisation had to be a *tabula rasa*, as he wrote in *The Wretched of the Earth*: you have to start anew with a new history.

hooks   Françoise Vergès, I saw many links between what you said and my paper. I talked about the recovery of the mother's body being to do with memory, and that the disappearing has to do with not wanting to engage memory and loss. Is there nostalgia in the deflecting away from mourning? I try to talk about *The Wretched of the Earth* as a very nostalgic text in many ways.

Vergès Fanon seemed afraid of depression. He took, as bell hooks says, a defensive position on the subject. He saw depression as a total loss rather than a moment through which one can work out some illusions. The reality of racism is 'depressive', and while he denounces this reality, he insists that it does not concern him: that he is a man among other men. Eduoard Glissant makes this distinction between *le pays rêvé* (dreamed country) and *le pays réel* (real country), speaking of Antillean intellectuals who cannot accept their countries and their peoples as they are and so re-imagine them: 'dream' them to fit their aspirations.[1] Fanon dreamed of a country where he would not be a nigger, and he was sad when he found that this country did not exist.

hooks Are we not all dreaming? I'm posing this in relation to where we want to go, beyond Fanon; how we work with him into the future. I want to take this back to the question of transnational humanism. What is the thing that we are dreaming? I was thinking last night about the ecstasy of ideas and wanting to be in this world without flesh; where the flesh has fallen away and there is no skin. Part of the failure of the imagination on all our parts in terms of a liberatory vision is that we don't know what we seek.

Vergès Certainly there is a liberatory dimension in the action of dreaming about a future freed of racism. But in Fanon's dream there is an ideal which is terrible to obtain in which he constructs a superego for the black man which has a persecutory dimension. This is the dream of a modernised masculinity, rid of that which Fanon considered the 'backward' characteristics of weakness, fragility and the heritage of western representations of colonised emasculation.

Fanon's analysis of black Antillean masculinity remains problematic because of his choice of a 'virile', modern, heroic, responsible model. In post-colonial psychiatry, we see the return of this analysis (though this was certainly not Fanon's project). The problems of Antillean society - domestic and sexual violence, criminality - are read through a grid which suggests that black men do not 'know how to be men'. European and Antillean (male) psychiatrists who have adopted this discourse contend that miscegenation and the organisation of the family around the mother weaken the role and function of the father (applying the Lacanian concepts of the name of the father and the symbolic and the imaginary strategically). An ideal masculinity, which responds to bourgeois norms of productivity, individualism and patriarchalism, is thus presented as 'the' masculinity.

Mercer Although you have been talking specifically about psychopolitics and the colonial administration, I think there is a metropolitan counterpart to the way in which Fanon has returned in terms of the politics of mental health. *The Empire Strikes Back*, a book which was published in 1982, had a whole range of work by people like Pratibha Parmar and Errol Lawrence that was about the politics of pathologisation, and how black families in particular are pathologised by the state.[2] Fanon did come back during the 1980s in work around building a critique of transcultural psychiatry. I'm raising this issue here because, although the welfare state does not exist any more, black people still go mad, yet this strand has not won out in cultural studies in the 80s and 90s. It has been displaced in favour of linguistic textualisation. The ugliness of the social and the way that black psyches disintegrate in social relations is almost intolerable. I think this work complements the work in Françoise Vergès' paper, in the same way that Jacqueline Rose's work on Bessie Head refers to the problematic issues around psychiatrisation. Sexuality is a front-line point of access to the colonised psyche. It is not simply an historical issue: it is very present.

Bhabha If Fanon does not want to see the relationship between biography and history, and at another level wants to deny memory, then what is the status of the notion of the dream? The dream of the black man is to be in the place of the white man, the dream of the black man is to leap, the dream of the native is to break: what is this ontological and rhetorical status of the dream, which he uses to talk about the future in the present? He uses it to deal with this notion of political hope. What is the dream? Is it just a metaphor, or is it actually rooted? I always thought it was actually rooted in a certain psychoanalytical understanding.

Vergès Fanon collapsed the dream and the real. When he interpreted dreams, he read them as the mirror of real events. There are dreams which are post-traumatic and in which individuals re-live their traumatism and victimisation. But dreams also register unconscious desire and fantasies that could be the accomplishments of this desire. In any case, what is important is that it is *you* who are dreaming: even in a dream in which you are a victim, you are the one who is producing the dream. In reality you may be a victim with absolutely no responsibility for the actions which victimise you; in a dream, you are the author - even if the events and representations in your dreams are connected with reality.

Bhabha   I don't know. I think he also uses it as a way of not wanting to think about history and biography. At the end of *The Wretched of the Earth*, in the chapter on madness and colonial war, he says that the native who wants to steal a date from a tree is in his political dream; this is his act of political agency; a real political act. There is something there about the psychic and the political which Fanon has not really worked out.

hooks   I was very intrigued by Françoise Vergès' invocation of the fraternity, because that was what I was trying to evoke with the word homophilia. Was this not Fanon's fantasy? I was thinking of it as the fantasy of the companion. Françoise Vergès talked about this in relation to mother/son. It seems to me that throughout our conversations there is an *impasse* around masculinity. Many of us have brought masculinity into these discussions as a key question of gender. Masculinity, as some of us have pointed out, is not outside the question of gender. I am hearing again the inability to imagine a redemptive masculinity that is not rooted in misogyny and is not rooted in the sense of the mother. If the biography that one cannot return to has to do with a sense of violence between mother and son, then how do we begin to reconceptualise masculinity in any way that frees black men from the repetition of this sentence of only being able to be free in a world where there are no women.

Audience   The discussion is beginning to deal with some of the complexities of the marginalised position of the black male that are expressed in Fanon's work. The discourse of black liberation politics has failed to address why Fanon's work was able to inspire the people who were most dehumanised and most marginalised within black communities. How was he able to link them up, rehumanise their spirit, give them that optimism and hope? If you look at the discourse around prison and prison life and the role of the black male culture within that, you often see that the introspection that you should have perhaps had when you were outside happens in prison. Why is it that you only get the chance to act like that in prison? Why have we not got these networks outside? There's plenty of work to be done in making those links between young black men: how to rehumanise the way they treat each other, how to rehumanise the respect they have for the rest of society and for the rest of their community. This is how we can use Fanon now, because he does articulate that anger, that misogyny, that sense of powerlessness. There is plenty of writing on the recovery of black women, of lesbians and gays, but black men are only beginning to build a dialogue with other marginalities.

Audience   I am slightly uncomfortable with the idea of Fanon not being interested in biography, because for a man living in the culture of the 1950s he was remarkably advanced in ideas to do with psychoanalysis, debates between negritude and revolution, Marxism and so on. Fanon confronted the problem of the individual in relation to history and is useful precisely because he reminds us of sameness rather than difference, of the possibilities of international struggle, the utopian element which is very difficult to maintain under the current political condition.

Mercer   I would like to re-flag my topic, which has been curiously absent in the discussion so far. Why does sodomy, or anal rape, come to acquire such an overdetermined and intolerable emotional significance in representations of colonisation? This requires more than an understanding of sexualisation in a Foucauldian sense, and the way in which, through slavery and imperialism, the black body is opened up for power, primarily through the gaze, by being constituted as a specular object for the other who is also the master. Why is it that in a black nationalist frame, particularly in African-American discourse, black men become homosexual as a result of sodomy experienced in prison? This is a way of disowning responsibility for the complexity of sexuality.

Vergès   Fanon always privileged trauma over fantasy. 'Fantasy' did not belong to his psychological vocabulary. With fantasy one admits that there is a psychic reality; there is a domain which resists total mastery and control, is heterogeneous and speaks in many voices. It is the construction of a narrative in which one's own desire is expressed. This domain cannot be assimilated to reality. With traumatism you are a victim: there is no conscious desire. One can attempt to find the source of the trauma which has wounded one's psyche and then find a cure.

Slavery was a traumatic event which wounded people's psyches and has left unconscious traces. Fanon extended the psychological consequences of this trauma to the entire psychological world of black people. Hence he treated desire between blacks and whites as essentially the consequence of trauma. The treatment of trauma belongs to medicine, with its therapeutic approach. To Fanon, trauma was also cured by political action.

Bhabha   Is trauma not represented fantasmatically? Isn't the life of trauma a psychic representation?

Mercer Isn't the whole point about trauma that it is unrepresentable?

Bhabha That does not mean that it doesn't have a fantasmatic structure. What Françoise Vergès is saying is that Fanon separates trauma from fantasy just as he separates biography from history as well as memory. Even though he uses dreams to talk about political agency, and he blends the different temporalities to produce a projected temporality, he somehow disavows this.

Vergès It is fundamental to understand the way in which Fanon brought politics into psychology. But it is also important to understand that his project remained contained within the institution of psychiatry. He thought that the psychiatric institution could help in the process of decolonisation in the colony and the post-colony, whereas to him psychoanalysis had no place.

Bhabha Everyone wants to be represented as being 'well' so that they might be fit to be citizens.

Julien Is there a way that we could return this discussion to some of the artworks within the *Mirage* exhibition, which call into question some of the categories which we talk about? For instance, the category of trauma as it is discussed in the work of Lyle Ashton Harris or Renée Green.

Mercer *Vis-à-vis* pathologising representations of the absent black father, one link I can make is in representations of black male subjectivity. Keith Piper's works of the late eighties such as *Go West Young Man or Father I Have Done Questionable Things* brought these issues into representation through an imagined dialogue amongst generations. Although her works are not in the show, I think Zarina Bhimji's work is about trauma in the context of the expulsion of settled Asian communities from East African states as a result of the Africanisation policies which were part of the decolonisation project pursued in the 60s and 70s. The unrepresentable loss - the lost object that is searched for amongst all the substitutes - all the part objects that are placed in glass boxes in the *I Will Always Be Here* installation - can be seen as relating to a lot of our discussions about memory and melancholia. Not that they depict trauma or the experience of trauma, but they bring the viewer into an affective relationship with that which resists representation.

Bhabha To particularise upon a figure that appears in two of the exhibits - The Hottentot Venus in the work of Lyle Ashton Harris and Renée Green - I always saw this as an extension of the colonial fetish both in terms of knowledge and the visual. But now perhaps we can read it in terms of a hystericisation of the body. Perhaps it is a projection of hysterics?

.

Saartje Baartman,
the 'Hottentot Venus'
from Sander Gilman
*Difference and Pathology:
Stereotypes of Sexuality,
Race and Madness*
(Cornell University Press, 1986)

1   See Eduoard Glissant, *Poétiques de la Relation* (Gallimard, Paris 1990).

2   See ed. Centre for Contemporary Cultural Studies, *The Empire Strikes Back: Race and Racism in 70s Britain* (Hutchinson, London 1982).

Artists' dialogue

Renée Green
Lyle Ashton Harris
Marc Latamie
Ntozake Shange
Homi K Bhabha
Stuart Hall
Gilane Tawadros
Members of the audience

Green It is difficult to be outside the central debate of a conference such as 'Working with Fanon' and marginalised to an 'artists' panel'. I'm curious about the role of such a panel and how it is perceived in relation to the theoretical discussion framework which has been presented. There's a certain power dynamic that occurs in terms of how the artists are positioned in relation to the formulation of the theoretical ideas which disturbs me. I would like to restructure this dynamic so that it doesn't feel like art is merely a decorative element - something that is tagged on to the 'heavier ideas'.

The work I have in *Mirage* (a work from 1990), reflects my interests in various discussions about the specular, and especially how these issues were taken up by some feminist discussions in Britain during the 1980s. In particular I was interested in the way that an artist (film-maker) and writer such as Laura Mulvey was trying to rethink the way in which certain ideas around visual pleasure were developed. I was also trying to figure out the way in which a body could be visualised, especially a black female body, yet address the complexity of reading that presence without relinquishing pleasure or history. I used a clinical engraved image of the Hottentot Venus, a combination of texts by critics of Josephine Baker and a nineteenth century traveller's text, an iconic and progressivley altered photographic image of Baker herself, a quote from Baker and a simulated toy circus with a revolving toy leopard. These elements in combination were intended to stimulate viewers into imaging in-between spaces: in-between what is said and what is not said and ways of being that didn't quite fit into what seemed to be the designated categories. To deal with those kinds of questions opens up the discussion in terms of being able to think about Fanon and areas with which he was trying to negotiate. Fanon had various positions: as a theorist, as a psychiatrist, as an artist in terms of the way he shaped his text. For myself I try to think of how I also occupy various kinds of positions; as a visual producer, as a theorist, as a critic, as a viewer and as a reader. All these things become part of trying to figure out what is going on.

Harris I agree with Renée Green. We have to find other ways of engaging and foregrounding dialogues around visuality and art production. Often there is a discussion around the work, without ever dealing with the material works themselves. A lot of the issues that have been raised at this conference are being explored by artists in the *Mirage* exhibition itself. What would it mean to ask people to talk about the work?

Renée Green
Revue (1990)
(detail)
mixed media installation
95 x 241 x 14"
Renée Green / Pat Hearn
Gallery, New York

Renée Green
Revue (1990)
(detail)
mixed media installation
95 x 241 x 14"
Renée Green / Pat Hearn
Gallery, New York

The dance of the Negresses is incredibly indecent....she gets into positions so lascivious, so lubricious that it's impossible to describe them....It's true that the Negresses don't appear to have the depraved intentions which one would imagine; it's a very old custom, which continues innocently in this country; so much so that one sees children of six performing this dance, certainly without knowing what they're leading up to.

Bhabha   In that context, it seems very interesting that there is this notion of the Hottentot Venus which in some ways circulates in Fanon's work: not as itself, but as a way of representing monstrosity and a kind of 'genitality'. I was interested in the way in which the work of Renée Green and Lyle Ashton Harris in their works on display in *Mirage* tried to both play and turn that image around. I wanted to explore how this might have come out of different understandings of that icon.

Harris   I am interested in returning to the idea of the body, and asking the body to speak with a vengeance. *Venus Hottentot 2000* is a collaboration between myself and artist Renée Valerie Cox. This reclaiming of the image of the Hottentot Venus is a way of exploring my psychic identification with the image at the level of spectacle. I am playing with what it means to be an African diasporic artist producing and selling work in a culture that is by and large narcissistically mired in the debasement and objectification of blackness. And yet, I see my work less as a didactic critique and more as an interrogation of the ambivalence around the body. Engaging the image of the Hottentot Venus has deepened my understanding of the body as a sight of trauma and excess.

Shange   The protagonist in my book *Liliane* is in fact a visual artist. She's trying to create, like bell hooks, a world in which the centre of the vortex is not in fact embedded in whiteness or maleness. As readers we experience her trouble via her psychoanalytical sessions that run in-between the narratives which take place at different times and in various voices that are both male and female. We constantly have to adjust our perception so that we can hear who is talking to us. If we mistake the voice, we're going to go on the wrong journey, and we can't take that journey in the wrong voice. So, there has to be an acuity and an alertness that I associate with the reality or actuality of the lives of people of colour: we've always had to know what white people were doing so that we could get out of the way or be in the way or be quiet or make noise; whatever we had to do to survive. White people, however, are the centre, so they can step on things and move things and destroy things and rename things and its done. We are seen as part of the landscape. But we can't allow that, so we develop special skills.

In terms of citing the wound or trauma that bell hooks has mentioned, Liliane does a lot of body painting and a lot of rituals that have to do with body fluids (menses, pollens, petals, leaves and dirt). She does these things in very sacred patriarchal places, like outside mosques and on church pews where they have said that we would defile everything. Liliane's works sometimes keep silent in the sense that they are temporary so you cannot see them and enjoy them and have them now. You can also not buy them. Because of the nature of women's relationship to men, and because we can be brought legally in terms of marriage and things like that, then we make art that you cannot buy - that you truly cannot have.

Harris   I want to comment on that by referring to my work in *Mirage*, which is entitled *The Good Life*. Although my grandfather was an economist at the Port Authority in New York City, he started shooting Ektachrome film in the 1940s and shot 10,000 slides of his family, his church community and friends for over four decades. In exploring his archive I became very interested in the different ways he and I portrayed the family. I see my project as an expansion of his documentation. For me *The Good Life* represents the return of the prodigal son. After having travelled to other places - spaces at once seductive yet hostile - which at times evoked a certain ambivalence towards my body and my blackness, I do see *The Good Life* as a return home, though not to a space where I'm asking for forgiveness but a homecoming that is mutually expansive.

To what extent is engaging in a calculated refusal a level of betrayal? To what extent has the notion of black masculinity betrayed femininity or has it betrayed us? Do we have access to international humanism? I'm interested in that but not as a second class citizen. I am interested in the extent to which my history and I have charted the ground.

Bhabha   How much, with the notion of the body, does the family come back into the whole range of theory, writing and art? Marc Latamie, your work is in a way more about a public history that you move into the studio. Is the concept of body and family, which is so much a part of the sugar plantations and its labour, part of your own thinking?

Latamie   Of course. The plantation is the reason we are in Martinique even though today, nobody understands why we are there because this question is not a natural question. For the piece I made for *Mirage* I worked with images of the last sugar factory in Martinique. I found it very interesting to see how this factory - which is still working perfectly - is trying to survive pressure from around the world regarding its product. In my studio it was really strange for me to work with sugar. I didn't want to raise the question of why sugar is

Marc Latamie
Galion #7 (1995)
Cibachrome
Marc Latamie

no longer one of the main products in Martinique or elsewhere in the Caribbean - I wanted to use the product itself to sculpt and play with. I wanted to see how the poetic side of the relation I could have with a material - which really was difficult to manage - could somehow be a response to my many questions. I went to the factory and asked people about their stories. I didn't do anything with these stories but simply took the product itself. It made me very uncomfortable at one point because they were expecting some response (probably after I had been there talking to them). Perhaps one day the work will return to Martinique and they will be able to understand more easily.

As artists, we spend time in the studio trying to build stories, trying to take the ego and put it there, deliberately misplace it; try to take something out and put it back in the studio. I cannot make a factory, I have no reason to make one. I try to force myself into the position of the traders. I ask them, 'why are you doing this?', 'why are you doing that?', 'Why are you moving tonnes of sugar every day?' I collect ethnographic material this way. I am of course very interested in Fanon's writing. When I went to the factory and told them that I wanted the sugar for a show in London about Frantz Fanon they said, 'Oh great we have two of Fanon's nephews working here', which was wonderful! Part of the family is still there.

Bhabha   What do you think about going into these archives and redefining them? The whole archiving of sugar in Martinique in Marc Latamie's case, in Lyle Ashton Harris' case the archive of the family. How do you recreate the archive and how important is it to do so?

Shange   Liliane undertook another project that might be what you are talking about. I had her gather a whole bunch of people of colour - Asians, Native Americans, Chicanos. They went on the side of the coast highway and they went up on the hill and they dug graves. They were all decorated in a huge mish-mash of regalia from all these different cultures and periods of time: a buffalo soldier who had his nose pierced, a Franciscan priest in drag and a rastafarian with green hair: you could recognise them but they were in the wrong body and the wrong space and time. These characters get in the graves and then Lili - naked with a rope hanging from her navel - would go and flag down cars on the highway and invite passers-by to come to the high mass for the dead ancestors of the coloured people and they would all lie there and the people would come and say it was wonderful and give donations and go away saying how beautiful black people were. But when they get up and put their regular clothes on, the same passers-by

Here we are working on Lili's new project: being the living tissue of lost ancestors in graves she digs along the Coast Highway where passing automobiles are flagged down to come to our funeral services which Lili officiates. We've got these feathers and cowries tied round our necks, faces painted, sometimes teeth too. We are wrapped like mummies or simply in loin-cloths. Lili is sometimes naked with one flower over her navel. Anyway people get out of their cars and come to our funeral. Our spirits are nourished by their visits and the ghosts of the New World get up and dance with the *gringo* enthusiasts: That is until we reveal ourselves as the not-so-well-off folks of color from the Mission that we are. Tu m'entiende that dead Aztecs are so less threatening than a live cholo. Plus we gotta watch for the CHP, who don't take kindly to us digging up public property for graves of live niggahs.

Ntozake Shange
From **Liliane**
Resurrection of the daughter
Methuen, London (1995)

are very scared of them because they are alive and they're not mythological and they're not relics. I think that's what you're talking about: we had to change how we are seen ourselves and be able to keep that alive in the world and not have it as something that just represents us. We can take charge of these things and define what's happening and put these other people in the landscape. Even though it appeared that we were dead and not taking charge of the world, we were in fact controlling what they could and could not do.

Green Different ideas have occurred in the discussions so far which have to do with the idea of home, body and the types of signifiers that the body has. A certain body (no pun intended) of my work was gathered under the name *World Tour*. The work, and other since, has involved a travel that is different from nomadism, but which has made it necessary to work and live in different locations. Questions that have to do with the idea of the self or identity seem incredibly fluid in these circumstances. I did a work in Antwerp called *Inventory of Clues* in which I wound over the floor of a wide white space several translations of a sentence that was supposed to have been uttered by someone diagnosed as schizophrenic, which had to do with the idea of being in a space when you know when you are in that space but you don't know the spot you're at ('I know where I am, but I do not feel as though I'm at the spot where I find myself.'[1]). I go back and forth between the translations that occur in terms of moving from place to place; the languages spoken in addition to the way in which you are translated as a body.

Bhabha There is something that Fanon would applaud you all for, which is your return to something which is called tradition (personal or public) and the way you then wrench it away - make it into something different. Renée Green, you have talked about finding yourself again. Others ask how this work can be political. In your practice is it very necessary to make a misrecognition in order to create another kind of recognition? Are you worried by people saying this is not really useful because it needs too sophisticated and subtle a perspective?

Green I think that disorientation is something that is part of my and many people's everyday existence. A variety of people that live in the world - to make a distinction between those who could be assumed to constitute an 'art conscious' public - have been able to find some sort of recognition in my work and the work functions in different registers. I can understand certain resistances to something that is not

Renée Green
Inventory of Clues (1993)
Details of mixed media
installation at exhibition
'on taking a normal
situation...',
MUHKA, Antwerp (1993)
Renée Green / Pat Hearn
Gallery, New York

one thing or the other - which is sometimes the case. Some people want it to be this or that, a commentary that usually comes from art critics. But it is possible to cite the experience of all kinds of people who are trying to live this everyday strangeness wherever home might be.

Latamie The question of being disorientated is, in the context of Fanon, part of language; talking from one part of civilisation. The immigrant in France, for example, is going to say, 'I'm nice, I have nothing to hide and somehow I will try to tell you who I am now if in fact you want to know'. It is a tricky question of dialogue, but I think it is also the point to which we have to return: this introspection; going back to the archive. I get into this introspection of the body in the national archives in Paris when I'm looking for little details of the connection between my ancestors from Africa coming to Martinique and why they did it. My memory was in Africa, I was born in Martinique, raised in France, had a mixed education, and discovered Africa when I was in Paris, although Paris didn't really accept Africa - and that was disturbing. The real vault of this archive is the Atlantic, the ocean.

Bhabha Lyle Ashton Harris, how did your family respond to your work?

Harris In drawing on the family I wasn't just drawing on my immediate or extended family but the imaginary historical family which would include Toussaint L'Ouverture, the Venus Hottentot, Michael Stewart and Jean-Michel Basquiat. I am drawn to the possibilities of these different levels of the familial, whether experienced or imagined. My entry into Fanon was in the concluding chapter of *Black Skin, White Masks* where he states 'In the world through which I travel I am endlessly creating myself'.[2] When bell hooks talks about moving beyond a 'calculated refusal', to what extent is she trying to extend the notion of family to embrace Fanon despite his contradictions? Fanon still offers her, as he does me, a politics of redemption. In terms of my own family's response, my grandfather really liked having his work in a gallery. *The Good Life* is so much about coming to terms with the fact that I have done a lot of psychic work for my family, often becoming the embodiment of an emotionality that exists in my immediate family.

Bhabha Ntozake Shange, we talked about the mantras of difference; race, gender, geopolitical situation etcetera. I am thinking about a way we might theorise the notion of survival, rather than tradition. The travelling, the generation of self through the archive and certain discursive practices, and generational difference. Generation is also about time, temporal lapse and temporal difference. When you need to reconstitute the archive you're doing it because you understand the potency of time and loss of image through time. What is the mediating notion of generation?

Shange   I'm a daughter of the black arts movement (even though they didn't know they were going to have a girl!). Previously, the self was very much negated: there was a black man or a black woman and the black masses, all of whom were fairly two-dimensional but very powerful. Enough to risk home and family for, even though you might not know who these people were. So generationally, as a descendant of this, I was very suspicious of this two-dimensionality. I have to feed the people but when I feed the people I can't give them rations, I have to give them a meal that's nurtured with love and that has particular spices for particular tastes. I'm very involved in the specific child, the specific black man and how he or she appears to him or herself. Because we could be seduced into the image of the other in the western world but we confront who we really are and make that something to be seduced by and worth fighting for, we have a different challenge altogether. This gives me a theoretical and ethical basis from which to move.

Audience   Homi Bhabha says that Fanon would be proud of this looking back to the past and referring to the archive. I think Fanon would be turning in his grave. If you look at the final chapter of *Black Skin, White Masks* he's very specifically saying that he feels no obligation to develop a black history; he feels no obligation to account for the past. He rejected previous humanisms (that which he called the European humanism or the white humanism) which were effectively exclusive, and is critical to the response to these, one of which is, 'No I'm not subhuman, I'm going to be like you'. The other response to this exclusivist humanism is to posit a new humanism. This is what I find inspiring about his work. He says there is a new humanity, there is a universalism, and that he does not feel obliged to posit a black history. I feel a part of the history of the world. Like in Toni Morrison's *Jazz* - 'I don't want to be a free nigger I want to be a free man'. In relation to the family, Fanon would also be turning in his grave: he's very clear when he says that the European family is 30% neurotic. He isn't trying to salvage or save the family. He explicitly refers to transcending the family. I think Fanon is in the tradition of universalism. I wonder how the artists feel that their work relates to that?

Lyle Ashton Harris
in collaboration with
Renée Valerie Cox
Venus Hottentot 2000 (1994)
Duraflex colour print, 16 x 20"
Lyle Ashton Harris / Jack Tilton
Gallery, New York

Latamie You can look through a window or you can try to open the door and get into the house. Personally I try to get into the house by the door: it's easier for me. In a sense Fanon never tried to say to people what he meant by universality. He came from Martinique; somewhere where we never deal with the question of universalism. We have to deal with a more pressing problem: basic communication. The reason why Fanon moved so fast from where he was to France, then to Algeria and then to Ghana, was because he had a sense of communication being the most important thing. It's not a question of trying to reduce Fanon: we are all open to discussions about him. We have to take Fanon the way he is and deal with him.

Shange ... and also to see him embodying an explosive set of ideas. I think in relation to the family what has not come up is his own ambivalence towards a mother over her initial rejection of him because of his being a darker hue. To what extent was his ambivalence towards women an ambivalence towards his mother? As opposed to replicating those systems of horror, our project is about teasing and taking them to the next level. I think he would be joyous in his grave: he would see this as an expansion.

Bhabha Because he's interested in the history of the present, Fanon continually works through events of the past, texts of the past, moments of the past. *Black Skin, White Masks* is full of it, as is *The Wretched of the Earth*. He's not interested in historicity - a teleological view of history - but it's wrong to say he's not interested in re-encountering certain historical moments. Indeed the whole way of conceiving what would be an anti-colonialist practice is based on beginning as he does to understand what is constituted by colonialism as a stage to the construction of another kind of historicity. So it's not just some kind of vacuous universalism. I think it's a very historical universalism.

Audience I'd hate people to think that because we're using terms like 'the body' and 'the family', we're using exclusively literal terms. Picking up on what Marc Latamie has said, there is a problem in translation, there is a problem in language. As someone who draws inspiration from Fanon's multidisciplinary literary style, the idea of *glissement* is something that we need to be aware of. If Lyle Ashton Harris sees himself as the embodiment of the emotionality of his family, I don't think that's a literal statement specifically to do with his family. It is also a statement about the artist as someone actively involved in a type of signification that creates symbolic meanings. This is not about filling in the gaps of the family tree, it's about looking at different types of perspective systems that have been created by the archives within our own family albums as well as through the media; and how we make sense of our movement from object to subject to citizen within all that.

Harris   I agree.

Latamie   This question of universalism is very complex for me. I never understand exactly what it means. The art world has borders, and so it is difficult to negotiate any such *glissement*. A few years ago, a big exhibition at the Centre Pompidou, *Les Magiciens de la Terre*, tried to resolve this question of universalism. There was an idealistic question in the air at this time, in 1989, about what was going on in some parts of the world. The curators went round the world and brought people's work back. The show displayed an idea of universalism, and six years after that show I'm still trying to see where I stand as a human being in the story that they created. I think it would be interesting to raise the question of Fanon with the curators of that exhibition.

Bhabha   Certain types of universalism translate as relativism. Marc Latamie has suggested an unsatisfied universal that keeps one working. It is not a question that something will be resolved. Fanon says that the struggle will take a long time.

Hall   I would like to thank Homi Bhabha for bringing us back to the question of universal humanism in a more troubled mode. I have not yet fully recovered from the staggering realisation that whenever the universal human is invoked, certain people had better duck because it isn't intended for them. They are not being inscribed, or they are being inscribed in a particular space within it. It's kind of an old space, but old as it is, I don't think its quite gone away and therefore we have to be quite clear about the terms with which we are trying to re-think that idea in the light of what Fanon might have said. That doesn't at all entail a kind of literal re-reading of Fanon because, unless I'm wrong in my own reading, I would say that this question is not resolved in his work. It remains unresolved each time, and each time he takes a slightly different point.

Bhabha   Fanon is reluctant to collude with a representational art which brings the history of the people back to themselves in recognisable figures. He seems very suspicious of that. In the same sense as the failed appeal of the universal, he says a fullness of representation of the people representing their past to themselves often happens around moments of struggle for independence. He feels this is of limited value; that returning the past to the present as some essentialist image ignores all the symbols, all the metaphors in the writing. The poetics of emergence in the anti-colonialist struggle must recognise the fact that the colonising period has also played its part in hybridising the culture. You cannot just go back to an original representational figurative or full notion of the past. He makes the same kind of injunctions against nationalist intellectuals who always say 'simplify the message for the people'. Fanon sees that people will be deeply intolerant of simplification and it is only by entering into a discourse of complexity that you can build up a revolutionary solidarity.

Tawadros I think what is interesting about the relationship between the visual and the textual in *Mirage* is that artists are not necessarily translating Fanon's texts visually but finding within the textuality of Fanon's work all kinds of possibilities about ambivalence, about multivocality: all these sorts of things which are within the many voices that make up Fanon. It would be interesting to try to untangle some of that and to talk about the way the visual works are drawn out of Fanon's textuality rather than translate them from the textual to the visual.

Harris ... and also to begin to theorise our resistance to the visual and our resistance to the work itself.

1 Roger Caillois, 'Mimicry and
Legendary Psychasthenia' in ed.
Annette Michelson, Rosalind Krauss,
Douglas Crimp and Joan Copjec,
October: The First Decade (MIT Press,
Cambridge, Mass. 1987) p 72.
Inventory of Clues was shown in *On
taking a normal situation...*, Museum
van Hedendaagse Kunst, Antwerpen
(MUHKA), Antwerp 1993.

2 Frantz Fanon, *Black Skin, White Masks*
(Pluto Press, London 1986) p 229.

Film-makers' dialogue

Mark Nash
Isaac Julien
Martina Attille
Raoul Peck
Homi K Bhabha

Nash   The trope of 100 years of cinema is also 100 years of cinema's relationship to colonialism and neo-colonialism. It is almost 100 years since the oldest film companies like Pathé Frères and the Lumière Brothers sent their film-makers out around the world to collect images from the colonised countries - images of the other which would change the way the other is thought about and represented today. It is still a very problematic relationship. Occasionally the camera crosses over, and instead of taking the position of neo-colonial power, it takes an oppositional position. Raoul Peck's film, *L'Homme sur les Quais*, which is included in the *Mirage* season, could be discussed in that capacity as could earlier movements when the camera was in a different position, like the documentary movement in the USA.

At the same time there is a problem about cinema: the cinema represented by the journal *Screen* for instance (of which Kobena Mercer lays the ghost in his paper). One of the things that was important about *Screen* was that it pointed out that there is something problematic about cinema, and our relationship to viewing. Oppositional cinema attempts to deal with some of these difficulties, which Brecht addressed, by looking to more dialogical forms: the viewer is in a passive relationship in the cinematic experience - how can strategies be developed to break that? A number of the films in the *Mirage* season construct a different type of audience-spectator relationship. Isaac Julien and I are currently working on a film about Fanon, *Frantz Fanon: Black Skin, White Mask*, which we will try to develop in a way that is Fanonian in structure. It is a challenge to extend philosophical work into cinema, but it's important to try, and to say something about Fanon's work today.

The Battle of Algiers, a film of the insurrection in Algeria in 1957, tells us something very useful about that time today, and shows it in great detail. It was commissioned by the Algerian Government after it had come into power, and was very popular when it was released in Britain in the 1960s. It's a film about a defeat. The director Gillo Pontecorvo wanted to create the people of Algiers as a mass collective subject - a description you also find in Brecht and Eisenstein. The scenes in the kasbah where women dress up so that they can get through the police lines connects with passages in Fanon where he talks about the role of the veil and national dress. In '*Algeria Unveiled*', his essay on the veil in *Studies in a Dying Colonialism*, it is not just what the veil does to the woman's face that is important but also the whole relationship to the body. In Algeria, the national dress can be used to conceal, so that in some newsreel footage you see women being searched by metal detectors for concealed weapons. We are interested in exploring the way that the veil functions both as repressive and as a source of resistance in the film.

Julien   In some ways one of the things that is very interesting in terms of making imagery, or of being interested in the idea of visualising theory, in my case theory around the black subject, is the way in which one comes back to the body. In *Black Skin, White Masks* Fanon's return to the body is of course an essential return. He returns to the place where scopic imperatives mark the body in a particular way which is part of a racist regime from which we cannot escape. I think it's the place of artists - and their concern with visuality - to also return us to the site of the body. I first came across this in 'The Other Question', an essay by Homi Bhabha which changed my life in terms of having access to making images and representations in different ways.[1] Fanon returns time and time again to the encounter with the white girl. We return to this in *Mirage* where we see the artists presenting their bodies and those of others. I think it's the look - the act of looking - that we want to challenge, to renew in terms of position: we need a third way of looking at the black body and how it is inscribed in these visual practices. For example, in Steve McQueen's work, the black male body is played out in a very particular way - a Fanonian way - in that it is disrupted, dis-normative. This is not only to do with the way that white subjects look at the body. It is also to do with the way we look at the body ourselves. I also think it's an important idea to investigate white subjects as well, to look in a different way.

Attille   One of the interesting things about making the film *Dreaming Rivers* was the opportunity to work with other visual practitioners in order to resolve ideas that hadn't been quite resolved intellectually. One of the most interesting areas for me is where western and African religions meet. I come from St Lucia. I play with the linkage between the dreams in the way the voodoo woman in the popular mythological representation of St Lucian culture interprets or has visions though dreams, and the way in which western psychoanalytic theory uses dreams. I cannot resolve those two things. The meeting of western culture and African culture, the surplus of meaning that this meeting creates and the way that meaning is sometimes misinterpreted is quite important to the way I work. What interests me fundamentally about Fanon is his pleasure in language, literature and images. He looks across a wide sweep of cultural ideas. For me that is very modern - to have someone from the Caribbean recognised as a transatlantic

Film stills from **Frantz Fanon:
Black Skin White Mask** (1995)
Dir. Isaac Julien
Prod. Mark Nash
Normal Films

consciousness. Not a USA Europe but a Caribbean Europe that is very particular. When I was in the United States earlier this year I realised that, although black culture recognises a certain unity in order to take us forward as a group of people who have shared cultural experience (thus producing a sense of benevolent cohesion around producing) there are quite a few significant cultural differences. The only way I could re-find ground was to close in to where I actually was - Tottenham N17, London, European Community - and thereby trace connections from that point. That process involves a whole series of class, gender and language negotiations which I find very exciting. Fanon's *Black Skin, White Masks* is a very important document in sustaining the value of work in a multi-disciplinary way.

The gender limits of Fanon are not insurmountable; Fanon is not a contemporary although he is a modernist. Here we have access to a whole series of discourses which allow us to do him the service of looking again in a way that he would allow us to do. I'm intrigued by the moments of rage in Fanon, I'm intrigued by the moments where he can't help be crazy about Mayotte Capécia. This rage intrigues me because Capécia's work was so well-received in Paris, and I wonder what the nature of the enthusiasm was considering the book featured a romance between a Caribbean woman and a white colonial officer. I wonder at the nature of the enchantment that the Parisians had with her text. I think there are strategic things that have to be done to bring Fanon in line with contemporary experience. Perhaps the translation should be looked at again. There's a phenomenal footnote in one of the sections in which Fanon mentions Capécia in the context of anti-Semitism. I wonder where that slippage in context comes from?

Bhabha bell hooks talked about a redemptive way of looking at gender, where the exclusion of women does not mean that the question of gender is written out. The footnote to which Kobena Mercer draws our attention in his paper points not only to the question of Fanon and women but also Fanon and homosexuality. Explicitly, the claim is that because there is no Oedipus complex or oedipality in Martinique, then there are no homosexuals.

Attille As Lola Young has said, the footnotes are quite intriguing because they are the points where Fanon relaxes and you feel that there's a possibility for getting inside his head. The point where he says that he doesn't know of any homosexuals in the Caribbean is something I've heard echoed in my own family background. But when pushed, people will say 'well actually...', and Fanon does the same: he says, 'well actually, there were men who dressed as women'. The whole debate around sexuality has allowed far more people to recognise homosexuality than would have previously.

Julien There is a way in Steve McQueen's work that you are returned to the black male body. There may be certain black male heterosexuals who will have a problem with the image of homosexuality. But the relationship to looking disrupts this moment.

Peck I don't feel at ease next to people who analyse the work of Fanon. I don't really want to analyse his work, as I would not want to analyse my own work in a theoretical manner. I consider myself on the other side. As an artist I want to show the complexity of things. I don't have the answers but am trying to find more questions. Hearing this discussion sometimes makes me want to block my ears so as not to be disturbed in my work.

Isaac Julien has talked about recreating images. I am totally in agreement with him on this topic. It is indeed an important time for us. We are part of a new generation that for the first time might have access to our own images. But I would not reduce this search for new images to a 'return to the body', which seems to me to be slightly narcissistic. I think there is much more than that in it for us. I see the different issues and work exposed here as complementary. We should not succumb to the seductive idea of the ultimate Fanonian interpretation or desacralisation.

Mark Nash has talked about 100 years of cinema and I think that's a tremendous legacy for us. We have not only to create and recreate something that we never had but we also have to de-create or deconstruct it.

As a film-maker, I'm not only trying to find a new and original way to tell my stories (for instance in a way that is not linear), but I also want to create new images - or, to take Isaac Julien's terminology, new bodies. But I cannot reduce my search to the theme of physicality that has been so dominant throughout this conference, or this new image of the 'black man'. The issues are much more complex, and there is much more existing bias. Either I fight this or I escape it. So, I have to decide how to direct my actors after so many years of ideas imposed by 'black' Hollywood. I have to decide how I am going to fight the existing clichés. Coming from Haiti, I know what I am talking about in this case, as Hollywood has created the cliché of voodoo that the general public knows. How am I going to deal with that in one film?

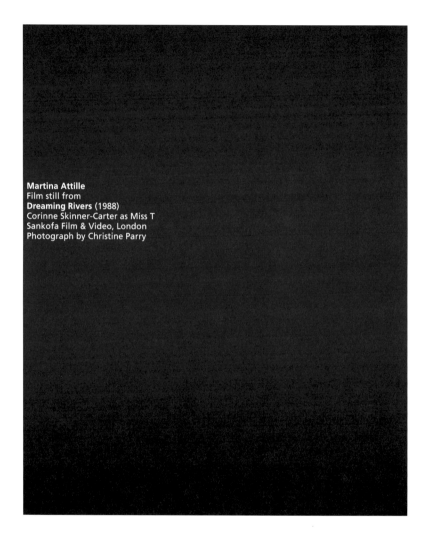

Martina Attille
Film still from
Dreaming Rivers (1988)
Corinne Skinner-Carter as Miss T
Sankofa Film & Video, London
Photograph by Christine Parry

How can I single-handedly counter at least 60 years of exotic and prejudiced imagery about voodoo? People (usually those fascinated by Hollywood imagery of the same) ask me why there are no voodoo scenes in my film *L'Homme sur les Quais*, when voodoo is such an important part of Haitian life. Its very difficult to work against that.

The same applies for all other aspects of film-making, including editing. It is hard to re-create or to find our own originality in the rhythm of our film. It is easy to say that African cinema is 'slow'. I see it as something different, as a search for a new approach, closer to our own experience. The same applies to our writing and our images. And this search continues in an environment that we don't control (yet), in an industry that is at best eurocentric. Sometimes I feel like a slave trying to evade slavery and find ways to deal with the master. Slaves always had to be one step ahead in the master's house for the sake of their own survival. The slave constantly had to anticipate the master's mood: 'Is he angry or happy today? What attitude should I take to counter his mood in order to survive?' This is exactly the way that the Haitian people are dealing with the American presence in their country today. They say 'yes' at first, but in the back of their minds they are already thinking of a way to get rid of them. This permanent *marronage* or subversion is an attitude I also have to use in my work today. We are in it and out of it at the same time.

Unlike most of my colleagues taking part in this dialogue, I have to deal with an art that is commercial and where hundreds of people are involved in decisions concerning my 'product'. This reduces my creative freedom quite a lot. I must stay aware of what the public wants (or what others think it wants). So through *marronage* I can try to fulfil all these expectations up to a point and try by the same token to break these expectations and find my own originality. I re-appropriate the whole of Western civilisation in all its success and in all its failures. I have to decipher it through the eyes of my own experience and my own history. To use the specific cinema genre of the Western as an example, imagine how the whole history of cinema might have been affected if the Indians had won the battle. Imagine the work involved in retranslating half a century of 'Cowboys and Indians' films through the eyes of a native American today. It is a life-long task. Adding to that, I have my own national and personal heritage to deal with, a heritage which my funders, financiers, and producers are probably not eager to address.

I read Fanon when I was very young. Then, having absorbed his ideas, I forgot about him. But he has been instrumental in my whole political development. I don't think that his work should be reduced to something he was not. The gender and sexuality issues that have dominated many dialogues are not fair to Fanon's legacy and impose a rather narrow agenda upon his work. Fanon's work emerged at a time of uprising, of the bloodiest colonialism, of war. Of course it reflects this historical environment. Thus, my relation to Fanon is more emotional than theoretical. I always think of him as a young doctor who was politically active - not just as an intellectual - and was always in the midst of activity. He was a French citizen involved in a liberation movement at a time when this was very unpopular. He died young, probably without achieving a third of what he might have produced. I keep asking myself what he would have written today, when even CNN is considered a leftist channel. His disappearance at so early an age moves me. My relationship with Fanon is with this tragic heritage.

Raoul Peck
still from
L'homme sur les Quais
Jennifer Zuban as Sarah
Velvet Film GmbH, Berlin

1   Homi K Bhabha, 'The Other
    Question' in *The Location of Culture:
    Stereotype, Discrimination and the
    Discourse of Colonialism* (Routledge,
    London 1994).

Dialogue

bell hooks
Lyle Ashton Harris
Gilane Tawadros
Homi K Bhabha
Members of the audience

hooks   The conference has made me think differently about whether the law of sadomasochistic master/slave relationships is, finally, infinitely more sexual, more pleasurable and more erotic than freedom and decolonisation, and that in fact this is the difficulty we have in moving towards some kind of liberatory vision; some kind of reconceptualisation of masculinity tied to the intensity of these images. Fanon focuses on the imperfections and perversions of love: 'Today, I believe in the possibility of love, that is why I endeavour to trace its imperfections, its perversions.' I'm interested in the idea of Fanon's gaze, and whether his work offers us the possibility of looking past that master/slave paradigm and back to what I would argue is another potential model of colonialism which is the parent/child relationship. This then allows us to look at the place of the female as coloniser. The coloniser is usually figured as the white male. This denies history. If we keep hold of this image then we do not get near anything that is useful to us in the present world of male and female colonisers and colonised. Is there a war of bondage that precludes a vision of freedom? Artworks that we have seen during the conference are about that.

Audience   I would like to affirm that the debate around representation has been moved on. The fact of nationalistic/fascistic thought, especially but not exclusively among black male communities, is a fact that needs to be addressed. It needs to be taken on board in discussions such as this. If we do not do this, then the debate that is entered into becomes completely impotent. We have talked very briefly about black male rape on other black men. Black men who are caught in a homophobic paradigm need to take on board the fact of their homophobia, and need to address the fact that in their past there have been instances of male sexual aggression towards males. They should not repress an aspect of their identity in this way. If black men can admit that there is a repressed, homophobic content to their history, that there is a homosexual memory that has been repressed, then they may come some way towards accepting the fact that homosexuality does not threaten them.

Harris   One of the things that intrigues me, particularly in *Black Skin, White Masks*, is Fanon's engagement with political autobiography. 'O my body, make of me always a man who questions!' Can we offer such a psychic engagement with our own bodies? Can the theorists who have spoken during this conference offer us such a thing?

Bhabha   I think that coherence about the body is in itself a problematic issue. The body is discursively constituted, but once you have said that it becomes less interesting. For me, what in the Fanonian spirit is most questing about the body is also most questioning about it. The questioning of the body is also its desires; what it searches for. At one level, this is a social question: one's body does not just quest and pulsate on its own, it quests in certain contexts: friendship, trust, confidence, loyalty, love, reciprocity, pleasure. It also quests for other things which have another kind of history and speed: it quests for caress, it quests as a father, it quests as a brother... I would take that phrase 'O my body, make of me always a man who questions!' and add to it: 'O my body, make of me always a man who questions *by listening and trying to transform the site in which my body also quests*'.

Tawadros   What is important about the range of visual art works, performances and films that are being presented as part of the ICA's *Mirage* season is that they are works which have gone beyond a point at which the work of art might be a residue of answers. They are made to pose questions. The works that are being presented here under the aegis of working with Fanon, that come out of Fanon's work, deal with ambivalence, with difficulty, with confrontation, with polyvocality. The 'space in-between' that has been mentioned is very important: it is a space which is between you and the work of art, something you have to negotiate. You are not necessarily going to resolve that space, or understand the work of art: there is not meaning there which you extricate. But it is a space which you are asked to enter and negotiate in various ways, meeting the work half way. Throughout the conference it could be said that there have been attempts to force a closure on Fanon, but that there has also been a lot of questioning. I am confused by a lot of things I have heard and I think that is excellent: I have been forced to problematise Fanon. This is also what art works are presented to do.

II

Day by Day...

With Frantz Fanon[1]

for Stuart Hall

> The springing wolf which wanted to devour everything at sight,
> and the rising gust of wind which was to have brought about a
> real revolution run the risk of becoming unrecognisable if the
> struggle continues: and continue it does.
>
> *Frantz Fanon. Spontaneity: Its Strength and Weakness*[2]

Why invoke Frantz Fanon today, quite out of historical context? Why
invoke Fanon when the ardour of emancipatory discourse has
seemingly yielded to fervent, ferocious pleas for the 'end of history',
the end of struggle? Why invoke Fanon who spoke most pertinently
and passionately at that historical moment when, as he argued, it was
a question of the Third world starting a new history of Man? No
useful answer can be made to these questions by simply pointing to
historical parallels, or by asking, accusingly, or self-righteously, 'who
carries the torch of struggle now? Where is the springing wolf in
sheep's clothing?'. Such piety misses the subtlety and the power of
Fanon's rhetorical emphasis on the singularity of the *day-to-day* - the
diurnal measure - in both struggle and survival. In *Spontaneity: Its
Strength and Weakness*, the understated phrase 'the struggle continues',
offers an elusive attempt to distinguish between what he calls 'the
historical law',[3] and his sense of the performance of the politics of the
day-to-day: 'the struggle for national liberation does not consist in
spanning the gap at one stride: the drama has to be played out in all its
difficulty every day... Day after day goes by'.[4] 'Historic examples', or
what Fanon calls the knowledge of the history of societies (his
example is the masquerade of the British granting colonial concessions
in Kenya) occupy the pedagogical realm of the political - a kind of
organisational 'ought' that is most useful in initiating insurrection
against the colonising forces, constituting a necessary bi-polar
antagonism. But the continuance of the struggle, the 'day-to-day', the
contingency of historical temporality and causality produce 'truths
that are only partial, limited, unstable... shades of meaning [that]
constitute dangers and drive wedges into the solid block of popular
opinion'.[5] It is this historical temporality that I would call the
emergency of the (insurgent) everyday, and Fanon associates it with
political subjects who are somehow outside the 'official' discourses of
the nationalist struggle. What. is particularly salient about the
temporality of *everyday emergency* is that it represents the *agency* of
insurgency and constitutes a counter-force to historical examplarity.
The temporality of the 'day-to-day' is what Fanon calls the 'knowledge
of the practice of action'.[6]

> The people will thus come to understand that national independence sheds light upon many facts that are sometimes divergent and antagonistic. Such a taking stock of the situation at this precise moment of the struggle is decisive, for it allows the people to pass from total, undiscriminating nationalism to social and economic awareness...[7]

Such a subaltern consciousness is constituted in three significant ways. Firstly, the day-to-day articulates the historical continuum of struggle as it takes place; takes stock of the situation as it straddles a temporality of transience, from which it seeks to formulate the knowledge of strategic political action. Secondly, the day-to-day is addressed to the heterogeneous, differential conditions and internal disjunctions - class, race, peasantry, the economy, oppression, exploitation, ethicality, generational difference - that constitute the liminal 'subject' or body of the colonised people in the performative act of insurgency; and, as such, it is less concerned with what I earlier described as the bi-polar antagonism between coloniser and colonised. Finally, the *emergent everyday* breaks down any utopian or 'essentialist' notion of a linear, continual development from a colonised person to a self-governing citizen. The (dis)illusion of such an organic, progressive transformation is, in Fanon's view, no more than the colonised desperately 'grasping the mirage of his muscles' own immediacy'.[8] Fanon insists, at least theoretically, on the need to posit a moment of caesura or negation in the recognition of historical freedom that cannot be sublated in emancipatory ardour.

For a writer and political activist, some of whose most salutary scenes of political engagement/encounter have typically happened while walking on the street (' "Look, a Negro!" ' being the seminal moment of racist recognition in *Black Skin, White Masks*), Fanon's emergent, insurgent day-to-day resembles Michel de Certeau's concept of 'local authority' as he elaborates it in his essay on the politics of the everyday, 'Walking in the City': a discourse of local authority compromises the 'univocality' of historicism, universalism or, in this case, nationalism. It functions as a 'crack in the system' that disturbs functionalist and totalitarian systems of signification and spaces of enunciation by inserting local authorities 'over and above' and 'in excess'.[9]

Continuance is not apocalyptic time, it is calculative time: the time of the day-to-day has to negotiate the undecidability, the indeterminacy of political direction (*the historical promise*) as it turns into a political or ethical 'affect' that situates the subjects' agency (*the political imperative*). The notion of continuance, as it relates to 'taking stock of the situation at the precise moment of struggle', is similar to that which Gramsci, in a famous passage on the subaltern subject, defines as the importance of knowing all the truths, even unpleasant ones which entails grasping the complex of superstructures in their rapid transience.[10] This is a form of contradiction, Gramsci informs us, that is often to be found *outside* the 'formally dialectical' which we readily deploy in materialist analyses. We need to grasp the dialectic in 'rapid transience': *as it is forming in the process of historical becoming itself.*

To grasp this everyday form of 'continuance' in the cataclysm of struggle - Fanon calls it 'living inside History'[11] - we have to eschew the springing wolf's instinct of total annihilation, and the messianic blast of the revolutionary gust of wind. But what are we left with, or are we, indeed, stranded? Fanonian 'continuance' is the temporality of the practice of action: its performativity or agency is constituted by its emphasis on the singularity of the 'local': an iterative structuring of the historical event and political pedagogy and an ethical sense constructed from truths that are partial, limited, unstable. Fanon's dialectic of the everyday is, most significantly, the emergency of a new historical and theoretical temporality generated by the process of revolutionary transience and transformation. It disrupts the hegemony of any 'organicist' or holistic social imaginary in the creation of the post-colonial national formation. Thus, the 'work' of political agency consists of negotiating a tension between the familiar bi-polar representation of the 'nationalist' anti-colonialist struggle, and articulating the incommensurable, 'singular' sites of difference that constitute the 'splitting' of the national subject at the precise moment of struggle. This should be grasped outside the 'formal dialectics' of a structure of recognition or consciousness based on the sublation of social antagonism or contradiction. Such an argument drives towards an insight that emerged out of Fanon's activism, and on his passing, serves as his most enduring, if problematic, epitaph. He argues that national consciousness, which is not nationalism, is the only thing that will give us an international dimension.

Fanon has introduced us to a dialectic disjunction between the discourse of historical, nationalist exemplarity and the temporality of the 'emergent everyday', in order to put before us, precisely, the possibility of thinking our way towards a national-internationalism (*trans*nationalism? globality?) without ethnic nationalisms. In Jacques Derrida's *The Spectres of Marx* we begin at the other end - with postcolonial and post-cold war inter-ethnic unrest and xenophobic nationalisms that haunt the history of the present. Derrida proposes that the constitution of a new internationalism - in the age of migration, minorities, the diasporic, displaced 'national' populations, refugees - demands a radical disjunction (as with Fanon) at the level of the ontology of national belonging.

Jacques Derrida's spectral and schematic comment on inter-ethnic wars in the new world order derives a peculiar post-colonial genealogy when read in the light of Fanon's argument. Derrida's comments are part of his ten word telegram on the 'new world order'. For an author who once sent us a *Post Card* five hundred pages long, it would be churlish not to listen to this mercifully brief missive. The public sphere of our time, Derrida argues, is articulated through 'techno-telemedia apparatus and new rhythms of information and communication'.[12] Their particular force lies in disturbing the assumptions of a *national ontopology*: that is, the specific binding of identity, location and locution/language that most commonly defines the particularity of an ethnic culture. In the event of postmodern media dis-locations, historical culture or ethnic 'affiliation' must now be thought through a problematic break in the indigenous, even endogenous, link between 'the ontological value of *present-being* - the political subject or cultural citizen - and its situation in a stable and presentable determination of locality, the topos of territory, native soil, city...'[13] Derrida suggests that the displacement anterior to the imaginary of national rootedness counteracts the ontopological tendency. For the 'imagined community' of nationhood 'is rooted first of all in the memory or anxiety of a displaced - or displaceable - population'.[14]

I want to focus on the enunciative and identificatory processes in the narrow passage *in-between* the discourse of rootedness, and the 'affect' of displacement. My interest lies in the transient intersection where the claims to national culture within the ontopological tradition (the presentness of the past and the stability of cultural or ethnic ontology) are touched - and are translated by - the interruptive and interrogative memory of the displaced or displaceable populations that inhabit the national imaginary - be they migrants, minorities, refugees or the colonised. At this conjuncture, the sign of 'cultural difference' or ethnic 'location' accedes to a kind of social and psychic *anxiety* at the heart of national-cultural identification. Its signifying articulation in our historical moment is, for Derrida, a kind of spectrality which is also a 'world-wide' spectatoriality; a 'bring[ing] to light, *at the same time there, where they were already there without being there.*[15] Suddenly, as in a shock recognition, Walter Benjamin's inauguration of the unconscious optics of modernity comes to mind, with its emphasis on acceleration and enlargement, so that 'the enlargement of a snapshot does not simply render more precise what in any case was visible, though unclear: it reveals entirely new structural formations of the subject'.[16] A space informed by the human consciousness gives way to a space informed by the unconscious (which is, of course, the problem of what it means for something to be there already without one being conscious of its being there).

It is by way of the process of erasure within exposure that a certain media temporality shuttles in an exhilic movement to make *at once* contiguous, and *in that flash* contingent, the realms of human consciousness and the unconscious, the discourses of history and psychoanalysis. It is this juxtapositional movement that interests me: this aiding and abetting but not necessarily adding up.

Despite a certain expediency on my part, I would like merely to suggest an initial analogy between the structure of anxiety and the process of ontopological crisis I have just outlined. As Freud describes it, anxiety (like ontopology) is a 'cathexis of longing... a defensive reaction to the felt loss (or displacement) of the object'.[17] What strikes me most forcefully is a certain continuity in the 'signifying articulation' of anxiety within the uncanny 'temporality' of global enunciation that I have described as acceleration or enlargement, and its signifying mediations; old/new, activism/atavism, memory/ performativity, unsatisfaction/dislocation. For the structure of anxiety participates in such an iterative and uncanny articulation: anxiety works through an 'expectation of the trauma' and a 'repetition of it in a mitigated form'.[18] Helpless in the original situation that is then repeated actively as signal in order to direct the course of memory and trauma, anxiety is at once the 'recall' of the situation - its memorial - and its performative anticipation or expectation. Anxiety keeps visible and present both the moment of nativity (or nationality) as trace and the displaced state of its objectlessness. In this sense, anxiety is a moment of transit or transition, where strangeness and contradiction cannot be negated, but have to be continually negotiated and 'worked through'. Anxiety is the mediatory moment between culture's sedimentation and its signifying displacement; its longing for place *and* its borderline existence, its 'objectlessness' that does not lack an objective, the tryst between territoriality and the memory of dissemination. Anxiety's asymptotic existence has rarely been more finely captured than in these lines by the late Chicago-Mysore poet A K Ramanujan, in a poem entitled *Anxiety*:

> Not Branchless as the *fear* tree...
> Not geometric as the parabolas of hope...
> Flames have only lungs. Water is all eyes.
> The earth has bone for muscle...
> *But anxiety... can find no metaphor to end it.*[19]

Anxiety stands as a borderline; as a frontier post that provides a space of representation/a strategy of reading that 'no longer concerns a distance rendering this or that absent, and then a rapprochement rendering this or that into presence'.[20] What occurs is a kind of 'laying bare of the substitutive structure itself',[21] so that the moment of the ontology of cultural identity comes obliquely face-to-face with the anxiety and memory of its displacement.

Such a rhetoric (and analytic) of anxiety is at once the symptom, and the substance, of much influential, current writing on the 'ethical' ethnography of the contemporary fate of cultural difference. In his Tanner lecture, 'The Uses of Diversity', Clifford Geertz tries to transform the traditional concept of 'cultural-as-self-containedness' with the estranging, ethical responsibility of encountering 'diversity' and thus engaging with a 'strangeness' or alterity, at the moment of its enunciation: 'to refocus our attention... and make us visible to ourselves' Geertz writes, 'by representing us and everyone else as cast into the midst of a world full of *irremovable strangeness* we can't keep clear of'.[22] The location of this strangeness is not the binary or polar difference between cultures, not (Geertz assures us) 'the distant tribe enfolded upon itself in coherent difference',[23] but a disjunctive, anxious terrain of 'sudden faults and dangerous passages'[24] that produces moral asymmetries within the boundary of a *we*, such that strangenesses are more oblique and shaded, less easily set off as anomalies 'scrambled together in ill-defined expanses, social spaces whose edges are unfixed, irregular, and difficult to locate'.[25] And then, that splendid summation: *'Foreignness does not start at the water's edge but at the skin's.'*[26]

Too true. But it is the amniotic structure of cultural spacing (a watery skin if ever there was one) - a 'difference' that is at once liminal and fluid - that Geertz cannot fully grasp as the *temporal movement that crosses between* the boundaries of cultural containment. The moral dilemmas arising from the communication and coexistence of cultural diversity are, within his argument, insistently represented in spatial metaphors that set the ground for 'puzzles of judgement'. Ill-defined expanses, social spaces whose edges are impossible to locate, uneven terrains, dangerous passages, clefts and contours: these are offered us as the ethnographic conditions of a new cultural episteme. Geertz spatialises the contingent, incomplete temporalities of ethical-political enunciation, describing a landscape of juxtaposed terrains of knowledge which install him in the archimedian position, meditating on the fact that 'the world is coming at each of its local points to look more like a Kuwaiti bazaar that like an English gentleman's club (to instance what, to my mind, perhaps because I have never been in either of them, are the polar cases)'.[27]

It is at this point of exotic *impasse*, where the 'mystery of difference' is located in the oil-rich 'excess' of the oriental souk, that Richard Rorty joins the argument, in his response to Geertz's lecture. Largely assenting to the world of diversity as a collage of juxtaposed differences - Kuwaiti bazaar and gentleman's club, Rorty admits that 'like Geertz, I have never been in a Kuwaiti bazaar (nor in an English gentleman's club)'.[28] The view from these unclubbable savants, which is beginning to sound distinctly like a most distinguished *salon de refusé*, is resolutely liberal-postmodern: suddenly the 'irremovable strangeness' of diversity becomes the everyday life of the liberal proceduralist. 'We can urge the construction of a world order whose model is a bazaar surrounded by lots and lots of exclusive private clubs', Rorty suggests, envisaging the postmodern bourgeois liberal ambling between the hagglings and equivocations of the bazaar and the moral equivalences and equanimities of the club, 'encouraging the diversity of doctrines and the plurality of conflicting and, indeed, incommensurable conceptions of the good'.[29]

As a postcolonial native, who learned his ethics in a Bombay bazaar and picked up his literature in what some (too hastily) consider to be an English gentlemen's club (Oxford), I see the relation between bazaar and club as antagonistic and ambivalent. Between them lies that anxious passage which in Fanon's terms is history as example, countered by the everyday as an instance of the emergent/emergency. For Derrida, this represents a crisis in the ontopological impulse: the instinct for location that, in the national imaginary, is based on the memory and anxiety of the displacement of peoples. As a bazaar person with some pretensions to the ivy-covered club, I take my lesson from E M Forster, who wrote the greatest of all novels about the complications between oriental bazaars and English clubs, *A Passage to India*:

There is no painting and scarcely any carving in the bazaars. The very wood seems made of mud, the inhabitants, of mud moving. So abased, so monotonous is everything that meets the eye, that when the Ganges comes down it might be expected to wash the excrescence back into the soil. Houses do fall, people are left drowned and rotting...

On the second rise is laid out the little civil station, and viewed hence Chanrapore appears to be a totally different place. It is a city of gardens. The toddy palms and neem trees and mangoes and pepul that were hidden behind the bazaars now become visible and in their turn hide the bazaars... They soar above the lower deposit to greet one another with branches and beckoning leaves, and to build a city for the birds. Especially after the rains do they screen what passes below, but at all times... they glorify the city to the English people who inhabit the rise, so the newcomers cannot believe it to be as meagre as it is described, and have to be driven down to acquire disillusionment.[30]

At first sight it seems that Forster employs a vertical dimension that guides the eye from the lowly mud-made bazaar, its inhabitants 'of mud-moving', to the European club; the civil station on the rise, in a city of gardens. But just as the self-containedness of cultures is being established, we are made aware of certain overlapping, oscillating energies that find no equivalence - the gravity of the Ganges that drives everything down, and the bird-filled trees that act as a glorifying lofty screen. But that is not all. The trail of alienation and anxiety is inscribed in the line of trees - the 'toddy palms and neem trees and mangoes and pepul that were hidden behind the bazaars'. They form a boundary that at once establishes the cultural ontopology and then displaces its enclosures and locations: the trees stand doubly-inscribed, at once screening and revealing, enclosing and disclosing. The fear trees provide an anxious passage through which the cultural divide derives its peculiar signifying space - like the Derridean *entre* - which stands between the oppositions and sows confusion between them at the same time. Such, then, are *'the fear tree[s]/... of naked roots and twigs/... not geometric as the parabolas'*.

In-between bazaar and club, the fear tree makes each site of 'difference' incomplete-to-itself, and therefore makes possible that great 'colonial' dialectical of mastery and misrecognition, sexuality and power, that creates *A Passage to India*. The procedures of 'rationalist' rationality and 'due' process break down irretrievably in both bazaar and club, in courtroom and civil station; the ever-evacuating anxious echo of the Marabar Caves puts paid to that. But having passed through the strait gate of the anxiety of cultural designation and alienation, the ethical relation seems to rebound back into the largely, though not exclusively, private and protected realm. Aziz reconstructs his personal life and spends much of his time at home, writing illogical poems on Oriental womanhood although, we are told, that in one poem he skips out motherhood and motherland, and goes straight to 'internationality'.[31] For Adela the lesson is learned on the surface of her body as her companion picks out the cactus thorns and in her anxious, some call it hysterical, delirium, she repeats endlessly: *'In space things touch, in time things part'.*[32]

If, so far, the analytic of anxiety has largely revealed a negotiation with the 'irremovable strangeness' of cultural difference, then, what of violence, of reparation? Let us return, in the spirit of Adela's words, to the fate of cultural and racial difference in the tryst of colonial space, and its historical and psychic affect.

Diana Fuss' *Identification Papers* attempts to 'take into account the multiple axes of difference that cross-cut, interfere with and mutually constitute each other... at the site of both fantasy and power' in Fanon's texts.[33] To this end, she engages the most traumatic kernel of Fanon's statement of postcolonial identification in *Black Skin, White Masks*: 'The Negro is not. Any more than the white man'.[34] I have written elsewhere of the immense, intrusive power with which the awe-full silence of the negative, 'The Negro is NOT.' - brutally, ungrammatically, peremptorily endstopped by the caesura, dismembers the dreams of a political imaginary based either on revolutionary victimage or nationalist narcissism.[35] By the time the sentence starts again, 'Any more than the white man', the colonised subject and psyche is totally laid bare, naked before the paradox of his own 'objectivity' in a strange way now neither black or white man, because the binary polarity of the colonial 'position' has lost its signifying 'difference'. The discursive and rhetorical expectation in the discourses of colonialism and racism, that 'black' and 'white' provide the grounds of a binary relation of cultural antagonism or cultural essentialism, is now disabled. Abjuring these alternatives, Fanon does not accede to an easy egalitarianism where white and black are somehow the 'same'. What we have here is a form of articulation that is no less violent, nor any more resolved than the complex juxtaposition of manichean 'difference' - 'zones... opposed but not in the service of a higher unity'[36] - that Fanon delineates as the historical specificity of colonial space. Negro and white are not so much 'equal' as they are equivocating, doubly inscribed signs of personhood, each 'less than itself' by virtue of its liminal articulation in/to the other. *No higher unity, says Fanon!* The manichean relation - to which I shall return in my discussion of violence and decolonisation - is analogous to the Lacanian notion of the coalescence and scission of the subject: 'A brief aside: when one is made into two, there is no going back on it. It can never revert to making one again, not even a new one. The *Aufhebung* [sublation] is one of those sweet dreams of philosophy'.[37]

Fuss's interpretation, quite appropriately, suggests that the colonial other is situated 'somewhere between difference and similitude... [for] any racial identity is organised through a play of identification and disidentification'.

> "The Negro is not. Any more than the white man". But "white" defines itself through a powerful and illusory fantasy of *escaping* the exclusionary practices of psychical identity formation. The coloniser *projects* what we might call identity's alienation effect onto the colonised who is *enjoined* to identify and disidentify simultaneously with the *same object*, to assimilate but not to incorporate, to approximate but not to displace. Further, in attempting to claim alterity entirely as its own, the imperial subject imposes upon all others, as conditions of their subjugation, an injunction to *mime* alterity.[38]

Fuss reconstructs the inter-play of colonial or racial identification and disidentification *as a narrative*, and it is the cogency of her account that opens up a range of important questions that relate to the interpellative and projective powers of 'whiteness'. Perhaps it is the narrational point of view - the 'injunction' of the imperial or white subject - that throws into relief the question of the 'agency' of fantasy and identification. Can 'whiteness', whose performative authority depends upon its fantasmatic staging, intentionalise the projective identification, or indeed the project of identification, within colonial subject formation? Fantasy itself, as a formation, is constituted through what Maria Torok, in *The Shell and the Kernel*, has described as 'an abrupt shift of level in the ego' which then leads to the temporal affect of the fantasmatic, the 'untimeliness' associated with its emergence and enunciation.[39] The intrusion of fantasy displaces the subject, drawing attention to its incongruity in the context of reality. It is the 'untimeliness' and abrupt shifting of levels within the ego which then enables a range of subject dis-positions - inversion, projection, negation: 'whiteness' as endangered and therefore violent, 'blackness' as silently passive and therefore potentially subversive. The fantasmatic may have a range of affects and political effects but it cannot be instrumentalised, nor can 'whiteness' as a projective fantasy be free of 'the exclusionary practices of psychical identity formation'.[40] It is this 'mis-fitting' of fantasy that articulates its power and its pleasure, and allows the acts of identification and disidentification the mobility and ambivalence they need to 'cathect' both the space of representation and the circulation or positions of 'address' that define the colonial relation. It is the disjunctive rather than injunctive structure of fantasy that makes possible the simultaneity of identification/disidentification, precisely because 'while remaining the seat of its actions, [in fantasy] the ego momentarily refuses to be its author'.[41]

The coloniser's antagonistic/ambivalent address of 'enjoinment' - 'to assimilate but not to incorporate, to approximate but not to displace'[42] - is a form of projection that cannot be narrativised in a way that instrumentalises the coloniser's intentionality 'project[ing]... enjoining... claiming alterity entirely as its own'.[43] In refusing to be the 'author', the fantasmatic structures the projector in/as a splitting 'causing the ego to give up its own self-government for a moment and to be content with observing its own vision like a spectator.[44] This gap between the enunciation of the projection and its 'surveillant' position is not, of course, self-reflexive: it is antinomic to the autonomy or authority of the ego, rendering it 'incapable of assuming responsibility for either the affect or the representation'.[45] Can the projective or fantasmatic 'object' - the whiteness of the gaze, the imperial subject - ever remain, in the process of identification, 'the same object' or the site of similitude? If we turn the tide of Fuss's account and read it from the perspective of its re-inscription in the return of the colonised gaze that is simultaneously assimilated and displaced, then the imperial subject as 'object' is articulated in a doubleness: the ego as self-governing and the ego as spectatorial. It is the oscillation between the two in the construction of fantasy that enables identification/disidentification specifically because the imperial subject cannot claim alterity entirely as its 'own'.

Alterity is not a property of the subject that can be 'known', nor can it be sublated. Alterity, as Slavoj Zizek has written of Lacan's *petit object a,* 'has no specular image and... as such precludes any relationship of empathy, of sympathetic recognition'.[46] Indeed, in the very performance of the imperial injunction 'to mime alterity', the fantasy of 'whiteness' or the sign of the imperial subject is itself involved in the drama of its own disjunction, its own displacement in the structure of identification. If, as Fuss argues, the choice presented to the colonised is 'be like me; don't be like me; be mimetically identical, be totally other',[47] then the coloniser, split between self-governing and spectatorship, is also cast in a moment of disidentification. The coloniser is no longer self-sufficient in the sign of 'whiteness'; in order to be projectively (and politically) powerful, it has to enter into a discourse of whiter-than-whiteness: a form of excessive or over-identification that turns the imperial subject around upon itself to face the *impassability* of its own desire. This uncanny objective of colonial authorisation - the whiter-than-white coloniser, confronted with the almost-but-not quite-white colonised racialised subject, is the colonial relation in its aphanistic moment. This is a movement beyond and different from the binarism of the objective and the subjective, for the subject is now confronted by the paradoxical nature of its own 'objecthood'. This is the point at which the colonial subject or discourse asks itself, in anxiety: whither white?

Can this psychic drama of proximity and violence ever lead to a form of regeneration or reparation? Of the manichean divisions of colonial space, Frantz Fanon has this to say:

> ... the zone where the natives live is not complementary to the zone inhabited by the settlers. The two zones are opposed, *but not in the service of a higher unity*. The settler's town is a strongly built town, all made of stone and steel... The settler's feet are never visible, except perhaps in the sea; but there you are never close enough to see them. His feet are protected by strong shoes... The native town is a hungry town, starved of bread, of meat, of shoes, of coal, of light. The native town is a crouching village, a town on its knees, a town wallowing in the mire.[48]

Thus at the very origin of Fanon's account of colonial space there figures an 'ontopological' split. The question of colonial 'time' has, therefore, to be thought in the interstices of the manichean division, in the refusal or impossibility of a transcendent or teleological temporality - for there is no 'higher unity'. How can we conceive of this boundary or borderline that neither sublates difference nor divides division in two? One answer lies in returning to the tension, or torsion, of historical examples and everyday emergency - this time addressed to the issue of subaltern agency as it emerges from the liminal conditions of manichean space.

Fanon fully acknowledges the importance of the desire for 'land' (the desire for ontopological belonging) as the most essential value, the most 'concrete symbol of bread and dignity'.[49] But in the performative process of revolution as action and agency, in the very search of equality and freedom, the native discovers 'that his life, his breath, his beating heart are the same as those of the settler... The Negro is not. Anymore than the white Man.' This problematic ethical-political proximity in the revolutionary struggle is itself antagonistic to - and spans across - the manichean compartments of the racial divide, setting the scene for the ethics of revolution.

Fanon's most fundamental and enigmatic statement on the 'ethics' of everyday emergency is this: 'the thing which has been colonized becomes human during the same process by which it frees itself'.[50] But the 'thing' is not simply coloniser and colonised. It is the historical relationality (the interstitial in-between) that defines and divides them into antagonistic subjects. The 'thing' is therefore not a binary relation; it is the taking up of a position, beyond the ontological consciousness of a Self or Other, in relation to the 'anxiety' of a liberatory history whose 'object' is only yet a trace, that still remains to be fulfilled. For, as Fanon explains, decolonisation starts for the native with a *tabula rasa* - a blank first page - on which is inscribed the 'complete disorder' of the desire of decolonisation. But this disorder is not simply a state of cataclysm or anarchy. It is, in some large part, the struggle articulating an 'unrecognisable' *becomingness* in the *being* of historical emancipation: it is the unstable and partial representation of historical necessity as transience that enunciates the ambivalence, even antagonism, between historical examples and the day-to-day strategic, calculative temporality. This is no less than the everyday struggle for survival and freedom after the wolf's last leap, and beyond the final gasp of the revolutionary gust of wind.

But what of the coloniser? The possibility of transformation from that position of dominance is also experienced as that which Fanon describes as the form of a terrifying future. So the struggle for the material historical consciousness of 'freedom' which eschews 'transcendence' (a higher unity) derives, out of violence, an ethics where equality insists on taking responsibility for the 'other' in the transformation of the 'thing'; in the anxious struggle for freedom.

> To wreck the colonial world is a mental picture of action which is very clear, very easy to understand and which may be assumed by each one of the individuals which constitute the colonized people.[51]

Fanon's image of an introjected agency - a form of mental action - as constituting the agency of violence is the fulfilment of a promise that languishes and lashes at the end of Black Skin, White Masks. The mental picture of an action could not be constituted in the repeated visual scenario of that book: 'Look a Negro!'. The statement appears early, and is then translated and threaded throughout most of its chapters. For instance, 'The Black Man has no ontological resistance in the eyes of the white man... and I had to meet the white man's eyes'.[52] And at the end of the book we find, once again, in the course of a discussion of Hegelian recognition, the notion that 'the slave turns towards the master and abandons the object'.[53] Fanon's staging of the racist gaze, which either crushes the subjected into a static, stereotyped 'objecthood' or causes the racially abused to experience a disoriented and dismembered bodily imago, has the overwhelming affect of a kind of Sartrean 'nausea'. Instead of action or its representational sign, it is the 'corporeal malediction' and its dissolution that is continually and nauseously repeated in Black Skin, White Masks.

Without minimising the remarkable phenomenological account of the racist assault - on humanity, historicity, culture - could we not ask whether this desire for 'ontological resistance' renders the subjecthood of the racialised or colonised person even more prone, non-actional and projected upon? Fanon's 'ontologised' desire for the recognition of a Negro or 'native' form of alienation or negation is indeed an impossible (and implausible) desire, for reasons similar to those which I described above as the 'specularisation' of alterity: for it is a demand to be conscious of the necessarily unconscious, non-imagistic processes of negation that constitutes the very basis of recognition and symbolic representation.

The 'I demand that notice be taken of my negating activity... [to establish] a world of reciprocal recognitions' further leads Fanon to the disavowal of psychic conflictual life for the Antilleans.[54] This occurs not because the 'psy-complex' emerges as a European designation of identity with the construction of disciplinary society, but because his ontological, universal man requires a homogeneous mode of culture and custom without the drama of sexual difference.

What is perhaps most significant is that he fails to read the homoerotic scopic charge that goes with the paranoiac structure of 'a man watching a man', which is his surveillant model of racist colonial recognition: the white man's eyes seek out the black man in a mis-recognition, whilst the black man seeks the white man's eyes for ontological recognition. In this relay of looks I read a process similar to Freud's transformative structure of paranoid projection, 'I a man love a man', that ends with 'He hates Me'. It is the ontological desire that will not allow Fanon to move away from the binary signifier in *Black Skin, White Masks*. In this case, the differences of gender or sexuality - with their ambivalent and cross-dressed desires - are disavowed in a hymn to the originary Adamic male body, black or white.

The manichean dialectic of colonial space and psyche that Fanon provides as the *mise-en-scène* of colonial violence and counter-violence must not be read as two separate, binary spaces. They are not to be sublated into a higher, third term (there is no universal man here!) because they must be read from the borderline that marks the passage between them. This splits the difference. It is violence that is the agent of this actionality, and its emergence is not, in the same sense, ontological. Fanon says;

> The disintegrating of the personality, this splitting and dissolution, all this fulfils a primordial function in the organism of the colonial world... violence, though kept on the surface in the colonial period, yet turns in the void... Now the problem is to lay hold of the violence which is changing direction.[55]

Of course we must heed Fanon carefully in 'On Violence', when he writes that the native's morality is very concrete: 'it is used to silence the settler's defiance, to break his flaunting violence; in a word, to put him out of the picture.'[56] But this is not Fanon's final frame. To understand his sense of ethical reparation, we must also comprehend, through the words of Levinas, the anxiety of proximity:

> An ethical relationship may exist between terms (or subjects) such as are united neither by a synthesis of understanding, nor by a relationship between subject and object, and yet where the one weighs or concerns or is meaningful to the other.[57]

In the final chapter of *The Wretched of the Earth*, 'Colonial War and Mental Disorders', Fanon produces a credo for the national and international relation:

From the moment you and your like are liquidated like so many dogs you have to retain your importance... You must therefore weigh as heavily as you can upon the body of your torturer in order that his soul, lost in some byway, may find itself once more... And then there is that overwhelming silence - but of course, the body cries out - that silence that overwhelms the torturer.[58]

Is this throwing of the weight of the one onto the other, this plot of proximity, a vindication of violence? Is the dice of freedom finally cast? It is the fate of our lives that we cannot choose, in most instances, those great apparatus of mediation that structure our symbolic world because they somehow pre-exist our presence. What we can and must do is wage our wars of 'recognition' in the knowledge that there is, in the midst of antagonism, the proximity of historical freedom and cultural survival. Overwhelm the torturer's silence and heed the body's cry!

1   This paper is a work-in-progress.

2   Frantz Fanon, *The Wretched of the Earth* ed. Constance Farrington (Grove Weidenfeld, New York 1991) p 140.

3   Frantz Fanon, *The Wretched of the Earth*, ibid p 142.

4   Frantz Fanon, *The Wretched of the Earth*, ibid p 141.

5   Frantz Fanon, *The Wretched of the Earth*, ibid p 146.

6   Frantz Fanon, *The Wretched of the Earth*, ibid p 147.

7   Frantz Fanon, *The Wretched of the Earth*, ibid p 144.

8   Frantz Fanon, *The Wretched of the Earth*, ibid p 138.

9   See Michel de Certeau, 'Walking in the City' in *The Practice of Everyday Life* (University of California Press, Berkeley 1984).

10 Antonio Gramsci in ed. David Forgacs, *A Gramsci Reader: Selected Writings 1916-1935* (Lawrence & Wishart, London 1988) p 197.

11 Frantz Fanon, *The Wretched of the Earth*, ibid p 147.

12 Jacques Derrida, *Spectres of Marx: The State of the Debt, The Work of Mourning and The New International* trans. Peggy Kamuf (Routledge, New York 1994) p79.

13 Jacques Derrida, ibid p 82.

14 Jacques Derrida, ibid p 83.

15 Jacques Derrida, ibid p 79. Emphasis Derrida's.

16 Jacques Derrida, *The Postcard: From Socrates and Beyond* trans. Alan Bass (University of Chicago Press, Chicago 1987) p236.

17 Sigmund Freud, *Inhibitions, Symptoms and Anxiety* trans. Alix

Strachey (WW Norton & Company, New York 1989) p 66.

18 Sigmund Freud, ibid p 102.

19 A K Ramanujan, 'Anxiety' in *Selected Poems* (Oxford University Press, Delhi 1976) p 11.

20 Jacques Derrida, *The Postcard: From Socrates and Beyond*, op cit p 321.

21 Jacques Derrida, *The Postcard: From Socrates and Beyond*, ibid p 321.

22 Clifford Geertz, 'The Uses of Diversity' in Michigan Quarterly Review vol 25 no 1 (winter 1986) p 121. Emphasis mine.

23 Clifford Geertz, ibid p 117.

24 Clifford Geertz, ibid p 119.

25 Clifford Geertz, ibid p 121.

26 Clifford Geertz, ibid p 112.

27 Clifford Geertz, ibid p 121.

28 Richard Rorty, 'On Ethnocentrism: A Reply to Clifford Geertz' in Michigan Quarterly Review vol 25 no 3 (summer 1986).

29 Richard Rorty, ibid p 532.

30 E M Forster, *A Passage to India*, (Harcourt Brace Jovanovich, New York 1952) pp 4-5.

31 E M Forster ibid p 329.

32 E M Forster, ibid p 214.

33 Diana Fuss, *The Identification Papers* (Routledge, New York 1995) p 148.

34 Frantz Fanon, *Black Skin, White Masks* (Grove Weidenfeld, New York 1967) p 231.

35 See Homi K Bhabha, 'Interrogating Identity: Frantz Fanon and the Postcolonial Prerogative' in *The Location of Culture* (Routledge, London 1994).

36 Frantz Fanon, *The Wretched of the Earth*, op cit p 38.

37   Jacques Lacan, *Feminine Sexuality*
     ed. Jacqueline Rose and Juliet
     Mitchell, trans. Jacqueline Rose
     (Macmillan, London 1987) p 156.

38   Diana Fuss, *The Identification Papers*,
     op cit p 147.

39   Maria Torok and Abraham Nicholas,
     The Shell and the Kernel, trans.
     Nicholas T Rand (University of
     Chicago Press, Chicago 1994) p 35.

40   Diana Fuss, *The Identification Papers*,
     op cit p 146.

41   Maria Torok and Abraham Nicholas,
     op cit p 34.

42   Diana Fuss, op cit p 146.

43   Diana Fuss, ibid p 146.

44   Maria Torok and Abraham Nicholas,
     op cit p 35.

45   Maria Torok and Abraham Nicholas,
     ibid p 35.

46   Slavoj Zizeck, *Supposing the Subject*,
     ed. Joan Copjec (Verso, New York
     1994) p 105.

47   Diana Fuss, *The Identification Papers*
     op cit p 146.

48   Frantz Fanon, *The Wretched of the
     Earth*, op cit pp 38-9. Emphasis mine.

49   Frantz Fanon, *The Wretched of the
     Earth*, ibid p 44.

50   Frantz Fanon, *The Wretched of the
     Earth*, ibid pp 36-7.

51   Frantz Fanon, *The Wretched of the
     Earth*, ibid pp 40-41.

52   Frantz Fanon, *Black Skin, White Masks*,
     op cit p 110.

53   Frantz Fanon, *Black Skin, White Masks*,
     ibid p 221.

54   Frantz Fanon, *Black Skin, White Masks*,
     ibid p 218.

55   Frantz Fanon, *The Wretched of the
     Earth*, op cit p 58.

56   Frantz Fanon, *The Wretched of the
     Earth*, ibid p 44.

57   Emmanuel Levinas, *Collected
     Philosophical Papers* trans. Alphonso
     Lingis (Martinus Nijhoff, Dordrecht
     1987) p 116. My interpretation.

58   Frantz Fanon, *The Wretched of the
     Earth*, op cit p 295.

Notes on Contributors

Martina Attille
Born in St Lucia and resident in London since 1961, Martina Attille is a film-maker and lecturer for whom representations of black women remain a central and complex narrative device. Continuing the proposition of her award-winning film *Dreaming Rivers* (1988), her current project, *Urban Loving*, seeks out a geography of desire specific to a local expression of time and space. Presently a member of the Black Women Artists' Study Group, established in 1995, Attille was formerly a founding member of Sankofa Film and Video Collective (1984). She has lectured at the University of California, San Diego, Duke University, North Carolina and Goldsmiths College, University of London.

Homi K Bhabha
Homi K Bhabha, Professor of English at the University of Chicago, has published and lectured widely in Britain and America over the past decade. Educated at the University of Bombay and the University of Oxford, Bhabha advises key arts institutions which include the Institute of Contemporary Arts London, the Institute of International Visual Arts London, the Whitney Museum of American Art, New York and the Rockefeller Foundation. He sits on the editorial board of, amongst others, October, the Oxford Literary Review, Third Text and New Formations, and is a regular contributor to Artforum. Bhabha's publications include *Nation and Narration* and *The Location of Culture* (both published by Routledge). He is currently preparing a new book entitled *A Measure of Dwelling*.

Renée Green
Renée Green was born in Cleveland, Ohio, and currently lives and works in New York. Recent solo shows include *Certain Miscellanies*, Stichting de Appel, Amsterdam 1996; *Mirage: Enigmas of Race, Difference and Desire*, ICA, London 1995; *Miscellaneous*, DAAD Gallery, Berlin 1995; *Taste Venue*, Pat Hearne Gallery, New York 1994; *World Tour*, Museum of Contemporary Art, Los Angeles 1993 and *Bequest*, Worcester Art Museum, Worcester MA 1991. Group shows include *Architectures of Display*, Architectural League of New York and Minetta Brook, New York 1995; *Installation: Selections from the Permanent Collection*, Museum of Contemporary Art, Los Angeles 1994 and the Whitney Museum of American Art Biennial, New York 1993.

Stuart Hall
Stuart Hall was born and educated in Jamaica before becoming a Rhodes Scholar at Oxford University. Former Director of the Centre for Cultural Studies at the University of Birmingham, he is currently Professor of Sociology at the Open University, Milton Keynes. Hall's research interests include political sociology, the media, race and ethnicity and cultural identity. Publications include *Resistance through Rituals, The Popular Arts, Policing the Crisis, Culture, Media, Language, Politics and Ideology, Reproducing Ideologies, The Hard Road to Renewal: Thatcherism and the Crisis of the Left* and the forthcoming *Race, Ethnicity, Nation: The Fatal Triangle* (Harvard University Press).

Lyle Ashton Harris

Lyle Ashton Harris currently lives and works in Los Angeles and New York. He has had solo exhibitions at the Margo Leavin Gallery, Los Angeles 1996; Jack Tilton Gallery, New York 1996; Centro De Arte Euroamericano, Caracas 1996; Jack Tilton Gallery, New York 1994; Schmidt Contemporary Art, New York 1994; Broadway Window at the New Museum of Contemporary Art, New York 1993; and Simon Watson's Living Room, New York 1993. Recent group shows include *Persona*, The Renaissance Society, Chicago 1996; *Face Value: American Portraits*, Wexner Center for the Arts, Columbus Ohio; *Narcissistic Disturbances*, Otis Gallery, Los Angeles 1995; *Masculine Masquerade*, MIT List Art Center, Boston 1995; *Mirage: Enigmas of Race, Difference and Desire*, ICA, London 1995; and *Black Male: Representations of Masculinity in Contemporary Art*, Whitney Museum of American Art 1994.

bell hooks

bell hooks is Distinguished Professor of English at City College in New York, as well as a writer, artist and cultural activist who speaks widely on issues of race, class, and gender. She is Associate Professor of English and Women's Studies at Oberlin College. She is author of *Outlaw Culture* (1994), *Teaching to Transgress: Education as the Practice of Freedom* (1993), *Black Looks: Race, Gender and Cultural Politics* (1992), *Yearning: Race, Gender and Culture* (1990), *Talking Back* (1989), *Feminist Theory: From Margin to Center* (1984) and *Killing Rage, Ending Racism* (1995).

Isaac Julien

Born in 1960, Isaac Julien was a founder member of Sankofa Film and Video Collective (1984) and is currently a Rockefeller Humanities Scholar at New York University's Center for Media, Culture and History. Julien's films and documentaries include *Frantz Fanon: Black Skin, White Mask*, 1995; *The Darker Side of Black*, 1994; *The Attendant*, 1992; *Black and White in Colour*, 1992; *Young Soul Rebels*, 1991; *Looking for Langston*, 1989; *The Passion for Remembrance*, 1986; and a four-part TV series, *The Question of Equality*, 1995.

Frantz Fanon: Black Skin, White Mask (1995) Dir. Isaac Julien, Prod. Mark Nash, Normal Films for the Arts Council of England and BBC Television. A short version of this film is available for distribution in North America from California Newsreel, 149 9th Street, San Francisco, California CA 94103 USA. In other territories please contact the Arts Council of England, Film and Video Broadcasting Department, 14 Great Peter Street, London SW1P 3NQ. An extended version of this film will be available from Normal Films, PO Box 3019 London WC1B 3PF UK.

Marc Latamie

Marc Latamie was born in Martinique and has lived and worked in New York since 1987. Recent exhibitions include *Mirage: Enigmas of Race, Difference and Desire*, ICA London 1995; Palau de la Vireina, Barcelona 1995; Fundacio 'La Caixa', Palma de Mallorca 1995; Nexus Art Center, Atlanta 1994; Saline Royale, Arc et Senans 1994; Gallerie Ekymose, Bordeaux 1991; Quai Grand Cargo, Fort-de-France, Martinique 1987.

Steve McQueen

Steve McQueen was born in London and studied at Goldsmiths College, University of London and The Tisch School of the Arts, New York University. Group exhibitions include *Foreign Body*, Kunstmuseum, Basel 1996; *Spellbound*, Hayward Gallery, London 1996; *Mirage: Enigmas of Race, Difference and Desire*, ICA, London 1995; *X/Y*, Musée National d'Art Moderne, Centre Georges Pompidou, Paris 1995; *The British Art Show*, Manchester and touring 1995; *Acting Out: The Body in Video, Then and Now*, Royal College of Art, London 1994.

Kobena Mercer

Kobena Mercer, formerly Assistant Professor in the Arts History and History of Consciousness programs at the University of California, Santa Cruz, now works as an independent writer and critic in London. He edited *Black Film, British Cinema* (ICA) and has contributed to many journals and critical anthologies including *Out There: Marginalisation and Contemporary Culture* (MIT Press) and *Cultural Studies* (Routledge). He is author of *Welcome to the Jungle: New Positions in Black Cultural Studies* (Routledge).

Mark Nash

Mark Nash was one-time editor of *Screen* and is currently working on a book on queer cinema and theory for the British Film Institute as a visiting scholar at New York University's Center for Media, Culture and History. In 1993 he directed a short film for the BFI, *Between Two Worlds*. He has produced Isaac Julien's *The Attendant* (1993) and *Frantz Fanon: Black Skin, White Mask* (1995).

Raoul Peck

Raoul Peck was born in Haiti and currently lives between Berlin, Paris and New York. He trained as an industrial economist, journalist and photographer before graduating from the Berlin Film and Television Academy where he now teaches. He is currently a Professor of Directing and Screen Writing at the Tisch School of the Arts, New York University. Full length films include *L'Homme sur les Quais* 1993, *Lumumba - death of a prophet* 1991 and *Haitian Corner* 1988. Short films include *Merry Christmas Deutschland* 1984, *Burial* 1983 and *De Cuba traigo un cantar* 1982.

Alan Read
Alan Read is Director of Talks at the Institute of Contemporary Arts, London. From 1983 to 1991 he was Director of Rotherhithe Theatre Workshop and is author of *Theatre and Everyday Life: An Ethics of Performance* (Routledge).

Ntozake Shange
Ntozake Shange was born in New Jersey, lives in Philadelphia and is author of plays, poetry and fictions including *for colored girls who have considered suicide/when the rainbow is enuf, Sassafras, Cypress and Indigo, Betsey Brown* and *Liliane* (Methuen). She teaches courses including the literature of people of colour, feminist aesthetics and writing and performance art at Rice University, Villanova and the Maryland Institute of Art.

Gilane Tawadros
Gilane Tawadros was born in Cairo and moved to Britain in 1970. She gained BA and MA degrees in History of Art at the University of Sussex, then studied film at the Sorbonne in Paris. Over the past seven years she has worked at a number of art and education institutions, most recently at the Photographers' Gallery, London, and the Hayward Gallery, London, where she managed the visual art education programmes. She is a member of Third Text's editorial advisory board and has written and lectured widely in contemporary art. In 1994 she was appointed the first Director of the Institute of International Visual Arts in London. Her forthcoming book on Sonia Boyce is to be published in 1996 (Kala Press).

Françoise Vergès
Françoise Vergès has written on colonial family romance and *métissage* in French colonialism and the Reunion Islands. Her PhD is in Political Science and she teaches at the University of Sussex. She recently collaborated on Isaac Julien's documentary, *Frantz Fanon: Black Skin, White Mask* (Normal Films for the Arts Council of England and BBC Television 1995) and is currently working on colonial and postcolonial psychiatric discourse and the institution. She is also working towards the creation of a Center of Research of the Indian Ocean.

Lola Young
Lola Young trained as a teacher in drama and acted for theatre and television before becoming Principal Lecturer and Course Leader in Media and Cultural Studies at Middlesex University. She writes widely on issues of representation, the arts and the media, and is a regular contributor to national newspapers and radio magazine programmes in Britain. Most recently she has contributed to *Reconstructing Womanhood, Reconstructing Feminism: Writings on Black Women* (ed. Delia Jarret Macaulay, pub. Routledge) and *Me - Jane: Masculinity, Movies and Women* (ed. Pat Kirkham and Jane Thumin, pub. Lawrence and Wishart). She is the author of *Fear of the Dark: Race, Gender and Sexuality in the Cinema* (Routledge).

Lyle Ashton Harris
In the world through
which I travel (1990)
black & white print,
editions 30 x 20", 72 x 48"
Lyle Ashton Harris / Jack
Tilton Gallery, New York

In the world through which I travel
I am endlessly creating myself — Frantz Fanon

Cover and frontispiece photograph of video still from the work *Five Easy Pieces* by Steve McQueen © the artist   Design by Yumi Matote, London   Printed by Cambridge University Press